Moments with Mary

Rhonda Zweber

ISBN: 979-8-43355-643-0

Contents

INTRODUCTION

Have you ever had moments that make you wonder why or how something or someone came to your mind? I'm sure you have. You may have brushed them off as a coincidence, but deep down, you wonder why those moments were placed in your heart and mind, and for what specific reason.

As our faith grows, we develop a clearer vision of what those moments really mean. We can identify those moments that God has given us to think of someone who may need a prayer said for them, to appreciate time with a friend, or to simply thank God for the beauty around us.

I have many moments like that throughout the day, specifically with thoughts of our Blessed Mother, Mary. There are several places in my home that remind me of her, whether they are statues of her, pictures of her, prayer cards, or the many rosaries that are found around the house. I also always wear a miraculous medal around my neck, and it reminds me that she is always with me.

I have become very aware over the past several years of how powerful praying the Rosary is; even just praying a Hail Mary has power to change things. As I ponder, like Mary did, about how many ways she comes to me throughout the day, I thought it would be helpful to share some of them with you, to help you become aware of her presence in your daily life.

I was diagnosed with breast cancer in 2007 and went through treatment for a full year, which was very successful. During that time, my faith life developed into a beautiful relationship with Jesus, something I never had prior to my diagnosis. I was raised Catholic. I never left the Church, but I was just going through the motions of a "good Catholic". I had no idea what I was missing. I have no doubt that God used that time in my life to prepare me for my diagnosis and to bring me home to Him. I will forever be grateful to have been able to recognize His plan for me. It certainly wasn't a "fluff" year, but it wasn't an awful one either. There were many blessings that I received which opened my eyes to the power of prayer and the understanding of just how much God loves me.

In June of 2013, our middle daughter, Hailey, invited me to join her to participate in the retreat called *33 Days to Morning Glory*. It is a way to learn how powerful our Blessed Mother is and how to deepen our relationship with her. In my case, it was how to create a relationship with her. I was excited to see what would come of the 33 days of the retreat and was looking forward to learning more about Mary. Hailey, my husband Val, and I began our retreat on June 13th so as to end on the Marian feast day of Our Lady of Mount Carmel on July 16th.

Without going into much detail about the retreat itself, I would like to invite you to check it out, and if you're reading this book, I believe you would really enjoy it! As we continued each day on the retreat, my relationship with Mary grew deeper and a devotion to her developed into a lovely friendship.

Once I realized how important Mary's presence was in my life, I kept her close to my heart. I knew as soon as I finished the retreat that I was going to do it again the following year at that same time. What happened just three days after my consecration would solidify the providential timing of my consecration to Jesus through Mary. I received a phone call from my nurse with news from the latest scans: the breast cancer had metastasized to my bones. As soon as

I heard those words, these words came to my heart, "Mary, I need you! Please stay with me!" That was the first time I had called on my heavenly momma for help, and I haven't stopped!

The following year, I invited several women from my prayer group to join me in the retreat, and we took turns hosting the weekly meetings at our homes. It was another wonderful experience. It was the same reading and the same questions, but I still learned a lot more about Mary and I saw her in a different light than I did just a year prior. I was in a different place in my life, just like most everybody is a year later.

My third year of re-consecrating myself to Mary included almost 40 people from our parish that I invited to join me. This was very exciting to see the variety of people who wanted to consecrate themselves to Jesus through the Blessed Mother. We learned so much from each other as we shared our experiences and thoughts about our readings.

The fourth year was difficult to complete due to health issues. My intention was to continue to read when I felt well, but I just couldn't.

In June of 2019, I was in a very anxious stage with many difficult events going on. I was having a tough time making time to pray even though I knew I should have been praying more. It finally came to me, while lying in bed having a conversation with the Blessed Mother, that I should be doing the *33 Days to Morning Glory* retreat. It was just a few days after the scheduled start date, but I found my book and began reading that very day. I made a deal with myself and Mary that I wouldn't put any pressure on myself to answer the questions but to just read and ponder and be with Mary for a short time every day. I missed a few days here and there, but I caught up on the readings on the days that I could read. It gave me the peace I needed in my day when I could spend time with Mary, and I appreciated her nudge to guide me to going through the retreat again.

I will refer to this consecration at different times throughout the book because it had such a profound effect on my relationship with Mary.

As you read, you will see that there are some short stories and some shorter stories and even some really short stories. I like to call them, a Minute with Mary, a Moment with Mary, and a Split Second with Mary.

Chapter 1

How to pray the rosary:

Begin with the Sign of the Cross.

Pray the Apostles' Creed while holding the crucifix.
Pray the Our Father.
Pray three Hail Mary's.
Pray the Glory Be.

Announce the first mystery, then pray the Our Father.
Pray ten Hail Mary's (called a decade).
Pray the Glory Be and the Fatima Prayer.

Before each decade, announce the next mystery, followed by the Our Father.

For each set of ten beads, pray ten Hail Mary's while meditating on the mystery.

After the five decades are completed, pray the Hail, Holy Queen.

Each of these prayers will be in the next chapters.

My earliest memory of hearing the rosary prayed was before Sunday mass as a child. Our family didn't get there early enough to pray the entire rosary, but I remember hearing people pray, kneeling with their rosaries dangling from their hands, as they responded in unison to a leader.

I was raised Catholic, meaning that I was baptized in the Catholic Church and went to church on Sundays with my seven siblings and my mom. My dad was raised Lutheran, but he didn't attend his church or ours, more than just a few times that I remember.

We did not pray the rosary as a family growing up and until just recently, I didn't know that my mom had been praying the rosary for as long as she could remember. In recent years, I would see her holding her rosary and praying silently before mass began.

The only praying that went on in our home was the prayer before meals and usually, just before the dinner meal. I don't even remember if I was taught how to pray the rosary as a child. The CCD classes I took had very little substance to them. We did crafts and we memorized prayers, but that was about it. I actually had no idea what being confirmed even meant in 4th grade when I received the sacrament. I have very little memory of it at all.

With eight children to raise, and a husband who wasn't Catholic, I'm sure it was very difficult for my mom to teach me the rosary. In those days, one's faith was something we did not talk about publicly, so that may have had something to do with it.

I knew Mary was the mother of Jesus and that she was so beautiful in every image I saw of her, but that was pretty much the extent of my knowledge of her when I was a child. It was a time when Mary wasn't known yet for how powerful her intercession was.

As I mentioned, my Catholic education included memorizing prayers. I knew how to pray most of the prayers that we pray during the rosary, but I simply recited the words without understanding the meaning behind them.

It really wasn't until I met my husband, Val, that I realized I may have been missing out on something pretty special. As our relationship developed, we talked more and more about our families and our childhood, and it was then that Val told me that his family prayed the rosary when he was a young boy. All eight kids and his parents would kneel around the huge, round coffee table in the living room during the month of May (the month of Mary) and during Lent to pray to our Blessed Mother. He remembers going to Mass with his grandparents and they would go early to pray the rosary with them. Even though that sounded like something I wanted for our family, the desire was not yet strong enough to pursue that once we had a family of our own.

CHAPTER 2

So, are you ready? Are you ready to unlock the multitude of graces that will flow when you pray the rosary? Hang on tight to your rosary beads! Here we go!

Sign of the cross:
In the name of the Father, and of the Son, and of the Holy Spirit, Amen.

Apostles' Creed:
I believe in God, the Father almighty, creator of heaven and earth. I believe in Jesus Christ, His only Son, Our Lord. He was conceived by the power of the Holy Spirit and born of the Virgin Mary. He suffered under Pontius Pilate, was crucified, died, and was buried. He descended to the dead. On the third day, He rose again. He ascended into heaven and is seated at the right hand of the Father. He will come to judge the living and the dead. I believe in the Holy Spirit, the Holy Catholic Church, the communion of saints, the forgiveness of sins, the resurrection of the body, and life everlasting. Amen.

†

I don't remember ever seeing a rosary in our house growing up, but when my mom was diagnosed with ovarian cancer in 2015, I found out that she prayed the rosary every day for most of her life. I thought it was pretty amazing that I never witnessed her praying it, but that was a time when there wasn't much talk about our faith.

She showed me a very old statue of Mary that was made of plastic that she had as a young girl. She told me that every May, she would make an altar for Mary decorated with wild flowers on it to honor her.

When mom made a trip of a lifetime to Rome in 1996, she brought back a rosary for each of her eight children and their spouses. I believe that was the first rosary I owned. Of course, as you have already read, I didn't know how to pray it at that time. I can't remember what kind of conversation I had with mom when she gave me the rosary. It didn't come up why she wanted us to have the rosary or that she had been praying it for over 50 years! I'm sure she thought that if her children would have a rosary, Mary would cover them in her mantle when they needed it. Or, at least know there was something special about those beaded sacramentals.

Hers was the first rosary given to me. Since then, I have received many rosaries as gifts from friends and family. Rosaries have been purchased from all over the world: Guatemala, China, Medjugorje, and more from Rome. One made from rose petals, one made from small shells, called "Job's tears", glass beads, plastic beads. Some are very elaborate, and some are quite simple. And one was made with beads that represent the months in which my family members were born.

†

On one of my many therapeutic visits to Goodwill, I came upon a wire cross that was made to place photos on it while

6

hanging on the wall. I instantly loved the beauty of the cross itself and thought I would hang it just as a piece of art. After I hung it, an idea came to me. I hung nine of my rosaries on it. It worked perfectly and I was tickled that I thought of this. Most likely, it was Mary's idea. I'm still pondering if I should hang a tiny tag on each rosary to help me remember who gave me each one. The cross hangs in our den where we spend most of our leisure time in and where we pray. Every time I glance at the cross, I remember each of the wonderfully generous friends and family members who have gifted me with such a powerful set of beads.

CHAPTER 3

Our Father:
Our Father, who art in heaven, hallowed be Thy name; Thy kingdom come, Thy will be done on earth as it is in heaven. Give us this day our daily bread; and forgive us our trespasses as we forgive those who trespass against us; and lead us not into temptation, but deliver us from evil. Amen.

Three Hail Mary's:
For the increase in Faith, Hope, and Charity:
Hail Mary, full of grace, the Lord is with thee. Blessed are thou among women, and blessed is the fruit of thy womb, Jesus. Holy Mary, Mother of God, pray for us sinners, now and at the hour of our death. Amen.

✝

Several years ago, a friend, Denise, called me one day and asked if she could stop over because she had something for me. She and her husband, Jay, came over and along with my husband, Val, the four of us sat at the dining room table.

I still had no idea what was going on, although I found out later that Val did.

Denise started telling us about her recent trip to Medjugorje and that she had been there a few times. Each time, she has had special rosaries made for people, which is what she brought me.

The rosary was beautiful, having different colored beads for each Hail Mary. I didn't notice the pattern of the beads until Denise explained what each one meant.

1st bead- Our Father- was a ruby, the birthstone for July, which signified my mom's birthday.

2nd bead- Hail Mary- was a tourmaline, the birthstone for October, which signified my dad's birthday.

3rd bead- Hail Mary- was garnet, the birthstone for January, which signified my mother-in-law, Loretta's birthday.

4th bead- Hail Mary- was an emerald, the birthstone for May, which signified my father-in-law, Val's birthday.

5th bead- Glory Be- was a pearl, the birthstone for June, which signified the month Val and I were married.

Each Our Father was a pearl. Every decade was the same sequence of birthstones, representing my family and repeating twice: Emerald-May: my birthday; Amethyst-February: Val's birthday; Emerald-May: daughter, Ashley's birthday; Peridot-August: daughter, Hailey's birthday; Pearl-June: daughter, Sally's birthday.

The medals that were attached were the miraculous medal, Sacred Heart of Jesus medal, St. Benedict medal, Our Lady of Mount Carmel medal, and a Medjugorje crucifix.

I was so humbled by the effort it took Denise to get our birthdays and anniversaries from Val and Val's effort, too! What a special gift! I got emotional at the love Denise had shown me. Not only did she have the rosary specially made for me, but she had it blessed and also asked several people to pray a rosary on it before she even gave it to me!

This rosary rests in a box right next to my chair in our den and I use this rosary every morning.

I was so moved by how special this rosary was that I wanted to have one made for each of our moms. We both have seven siblings and with two parents and eight kids, the decades worked perfectly. Denise was able to have them specially made and I gave them to my mom and mother-in-law, Loretta, the following Christmas, but not before I had prayed a rosary on each for them.

So, we always pray the first four beads for our parents.

CHAPTER 4

Glory Be:
Glory be to the Father, and to the Son, and to the Holy Spirit. As it was in the beginning, is now, and ever shall be, world without end. Amen.

Fatima Prayer:
O my Jesus, forgive us our sins, save us from the fires of hell. Lead all souls to heaven, especially those who have most need of your mercy.

✝

Our oldest daughter, Ashley, had the opportunity to study abroad for the fall semester in Rome. It was at that time, when Val and I began praying the rosary together and we offered it for her. Val and I were very blessed to have been able to visit Ashley abroad. While we were there, something absolutely amazing happened. The three of us were sitting on the terrace, just outside our room at the place where we were staying, and Ash was showing us the gifts she bought when she traveled to Lourdes, France. Ashley and her friends were there on the weekend of the Feast of the Immaculate Conception. She began showing us the dozen or so small bottles of holy water that she brought back and one large bottle that was only a third full. She said that she was limited on how much holy water she could put in the bottle.

The next package that Ashley unwrapped was full of medals of several saints. There were Miraculous Medals, a medal of St. Francis, a medal of Pope Francis, and a few others. They were all so beautiful, and she offered one to me. I asked if I could have a smaller medal of Mary that had a special blue background on it. I added it to my chain that already had a medal from Medjugorje. Ashley sorted the medals and talked about who might like each one.

Finally, Ashley took a package that was wrapped in two types of paper. As she held it in her hand, she began telling the story about how she came to buy this gift for me. She said that she saw a small statue of our Blessed Mother at a store that was pink and had glitter on it. She thought I would like the pink one because of my love of pink. She decided to pass on the first statue that she saw but when she saw another Mary that was also pink, she decided to buy that one for me. As she was telling us how she came to choose the Mary that she was unwrapping, she looked down at the statue and her mouth dropped open and her eyes grew very big. Val and I had no idea what was going on, so we waited for Ashley to be able to speak. Once she did, her words were, at first, difficult to believe.

She told us that she bought a pink Virgin Mary, but she opened up her package and showed us that Mary was blue. There was no sign of any pink in the package. Even the glitter that had fallen off of the statue in the wrapper was blue. To be honest, I thought she was just kidding us, but it soon was clear that she was not. I asked if she saw the salesperson wrap the pink statue which she did. I asked if she had seen it pink again before that day. She said that she came home from the trip and showed her friends, and it was pink. It had been in the simple plastic bag with the Holy water and medals for the past three weeks, untouched until that moment.

For several minutes, we tried to reason why the statue was pink and then was blue. But there wasn't any explanation except the possibility that Mary interceded for some reason. We just needed to figure out what it was. I considered that the CT scan and the bone scan that I was having when we got back from our trip, were going to have miraculous results. We agreed that would be a pretty cool intercession. Ashley wanted to tell her friends. Everyone was amazed at the story and the sight of our Blessed Mother that was definitely blue.

When we returned from our trip, I had an appointment with my oncologist to go over the results of scans on my bones (where the cancer had recently moved to at that time) that I had done before our trip. Depending on the results, I was planning on continuing with my chemo after the appointment. As my doctor went over my chart and showed me my lab results and the findings of both scans, she was a bit perplexed as she read the words, "there is no scintigraphic evidence for active skeletal metastases" in my bones. I asked her to use words that I could tell my family that they would understand better. She paraphrased, "there is no metabolic activity in your bones."

If I understood her correctly, that meant that there wasn't anything going on in my bones, definitely no new cancer cells. She even added that there was no sign of arthritis either, something I hadn't given any thought to but was pleased when she told me.

From the CT scan to check my stomach lining (which is where the cancer had moved most recently), the results were just as surprising. When I was first told that my stomach lining had thickened due to the chemo I had, I was told that the thickness would never reverse. Guess what? The apparent stomach wall thickening appeared "improved" and my doctor added that there was less cancer activity there, too!

I asked my doctor what she thought of the results, and she said that she did not expect to see such great results AND she didn't think that the chemo that I had been on would have been effective as long as it had. Well, she didn't know about Mary's intercession! So, I had to tell her the story. She left the room with a smile on her face and I'm sure she was giving some thought to what I had just told her.

That did not mean that my cancer was gone, but it was a very good sign that it was going in the right direction. I was told that I would probably never be cancer-free again and our goal was to keep the cancer cells from multiplying and moving, and we were doing a pretty good job at that!

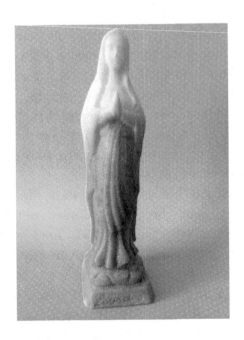

CHAPTER 5

The Joyful Mysteries

The events surrounding the coming of Our Lord, God made man, are cause for intense joy. We meditate on these mysteries asking Our Lady to help us discover the secret of Christian joy- the coming of Our Lord Jesus Christ in the flesh.

The Joyful Mysteries are prayed on Mondays and Saturdays.

✝

The Joyful Mysteries are my favorite because, well, they are full of joy, and that's the kind of life I want to live: a joy-filled one. Joy is an adjective used often when people describe me. I say this with humility and also in thanksgiving for the grace I've received to be filled with joy even though I have been carrying the cross of cancer for many years. That grace, I believe has come from my relationship with Mary. I remember Val telling me that he saw a difference in me after my consecration through *33 Days to Morning Glory*. I don't remember if he could identify it with words, but he noticed a change in me. The best that he could describe it was that I became more of a servant, and I was more peaceful.

✝

After receiving my statue of Mary from Ashley, I began sharing with anyone who would listen, the way she changed color and I guess the word got out because when I was at a retreat, a woman asked me if she could see my statue. Because we live right next door to our church, I was able to go home and get the statue. Kathy, who is co-owner of Holy Cross Books and Gifts store, was enamored with my statue and believed there was something I was supposed to be doing with the special statue. I told her I was open to it. After she prayed about it for a while, she contacted me and asked if I would come to her store and speak to a small group of people who had a devotion to Mary. I gave Kathy my fiat, my yes, just like Mary did.

I was blessed with several opportunities to speak to about a dozen patrons of the store about my special statue. I would bring the statue and talk about my journey of cancer through the Joyful Mysteries. I will share some of those thoughts throughout the next chapters of the Joyful Mysteries.

†

Val's grandma was an amazing prayer warrior. From the time I married into the family, she had been praying for me. With each baby born, she added the girls to her prayers. What made her prayers so special was that she prayed a specific decade of the rosary for EACH of us and then send us a card with the Mystery of the Rosary that she prayed, the decade that she prayed, and the date and time that she prayed it! She didn't do this just for our family; she did it for ALL of her children, grandchildren and great-grandchildren! She prayed all day, every day! I still have the cards that she sent us with all of the information in her handwriting, which is also very special to have. She prayed for us, even as she was into her early 90's, until her memory began to fade. That doesn't mean she stopped praying, by any means. I am sure she continued to pray for all of us until she passed away at 97, with her children surrounding her. She took her final breath as her family completed, you guessed it, the rosary.

†

Val prays his morning rosary on the green (Irish) rosary that was purchased with money that his grandma gave him.

CHAPTER 6

The First Joyful Mystery
The Annunciation

The angel Gabriel was sent from God to a city of Galilee named Nazareth, to a virgin betrothed to a man whose name was Joseph...And he came to her and said, "Hail, full of grace, the Lord is with you!" (Luke 1:26-28)

Dear Mother Mary, please help us to say *yes* to God's plan for us, just as you did, and help us do something remarkable in our life by serving Him with humble hearts.

Fruit of the Mystery: Humility

Our Father

†

Shortly after committing to spending an hour with Jesus in Eucharistic Adoration, the family who shared the hour with me began praying the rosary out loud during our hour. That family lived next door to us at the time, and their two youngest children, Aaron and Joe, were about four and eight years old. They also have a daughter who was 12 and would often join the family.

The first several times, the family would pray the rosary with each family member praying a decade. The father, Mike, would lead first. Then the boys would have their turn. Joe, (4) would do the best he could at praying the Hail Mary, with some of his words not quite right, but so adorable. Sometimes, his mom and dad would guide him a bit, but most of the time I was completely impressed with the foundation that Mike and Renee instilled into their family and at such a young age. Joe's voice was tiny, but it had determination as he prayed the Hail Mary. Most of the time, I smiled throughout his decade as I watched him squirm and fidget on his kneeler as he prayed. Aaron (8) did a very nice job at remembering the mystery of the rosary and he didn't need any help praying and keeping track of the Hail Mary's.

At one point, Mike asked me if I would like to pray a decade of the rosary. At first, I panicked because I didn't know how to pray the rosary without looking at the pamphlet, which I would always have with me to refer to. Mike's invitation to pray with them encouraged me to step out of my comfort zone and into a place where I was meant to be.

✝

Another time when I tasted a piece of humble pie was when I was part of the Rosary Making Ministry at my parish. I know, right? I still didn't know how to pray the rosary, but I learned how to string the beads and tie the knots. Maybe that was Mary's way of nudging me toward her. One of the things that the ministry does is teach the third graders at our parish school, how to make a rosary for them to keep. They chose the color of beads, counted out five sets of ten beads, and then strung them. We would tie the knots and add the crucifix and medal and the five extra beads between them.

This is where the humble pie comes in. One student I was helping was all ready for me to add the last beads, the medal, and the crucifix. Since I didn't know what the prayers were, I did not put the correct number of beads on. I was embarrassed to admit that I made the rosary incorrectly, and because I had tied all of the knots, I didn't say anything! AHHHH! I can't believe I did that! I hope I didn't damage that student's learning of the rosary because of my pride!

✝

Ten Hail Mary's

CHAPTER 7

The Second Joyful Mystery
The Visitation

In those days Mary arose and went with haste into the hill country, to a city of Judah... And when Elizabeth heard the greeting of Mary, the child leaped in her womb. (Luke 1:39-41)

Dear Mother Mary, please open our hearts to feel your presence in our lives so we can reach out to our neighbors and feel the same joy that it brought Elizabeth.

Fruit of the Mystery: Love of Neighbor

Our Father

✝

Do you remember the story about the angel Gabriel appearing to Zechariah and telling him that his wife, Elizabeth, would bear a son, even in her advanced years? She would name that son John, "And you will have joy and gladness and many will rejoice at his birth." (Luke 1:14). That story brings me back to 2001. I was sitting in the first pew at church, listening to this story from the Gospel of Luke. Never before had I "heard" the words that were read and never before had words hit home as closely as they did that day.

I let the words seep into my heart and tears came to my eyes. I smiled, realizing that a prayer of mine had just been answered. Val and I had been wondering if we were to have any more children and being "advanced in years" at 37, I wasn't sure it was going to happen. We certainly wanted to have more children but as my doctor told me, "Your eggs have been sitting on the shelf for a while." I honestly don't remember if I prayed for another baby or just wondered if I would have one, but when I heard that Elizabeth was to have a baby in her old age, I knew at that moment that God planned for us to have another baby.

I find connections with many things in my life and that definitely was one of them. But that wasn't the only God-incidence. I found another parallel between Elizabeth and me because my confirmation name is Elizabeth.

Later, when I was pregnant, Val and I were discussing names for the baby. We never wanted to find out what the sex of the babies were, so we would choose a boy's name and a girl's name. Just for the record, Ashley would have been Nathan and Hailey would have been Joshua. I will give you one guess as to which name we chose if Sally would have been a boy....... You got it! JOHN!

Sally has brought us great gladness and much joy, and she was definitely in God's plan for our family. It was NO accident that she arrived on June 18, 2002. It was Val's and my 9th wedding anniversary. What a gift!

Oh yeah, she weighed in at exactly 9 pounds!

✝

We have a framed image of "Jump for Joy" hanging in our den and whenever we pray the joyful mysteries, especially the Visitation, I look at that image and just smile inside, imagining what it must have felt like to feel the babies leap in the wombs of these two mothers.

†

Ashley and Danny received a small statue of Our Lady of Fatima from a friend as a wedding gift in May of 2017. It looked similar to my statue of Our Lady of Lourdes, probably made out of the same material with the glitter covering part of her body but her color was an aquamarine and was much more vibrant and shiny.

Less than two months later, Ashley sent me a video that showed that her statue had changed color! The color still had a touch of blue in it, but it was mostly a fuchsia color.

One day at daily mass, a line stood out to me, "And how does it happen that the mother of my Lord should come to me?" Elizabeth knew Mary was carrying our Savior, Jesus! I didn't realize that the Holy Spirit told Elizabeth as well!

Fr. Tom spoke about how the two mothers didn't know what was ahead for their sons but were still joyful in the moment.

†

Ten Hail Mary's

CHAPTER 8

The Third Joyful Mystery
The Birth of Jesus

And she gave birth to her first-born Son and wrapped him in swaddling clothes, and laid him in a manger, because there was no room for them in the inn. (*Luke 2:7*)

Dear Mother Mary, please give us the grace to enjoy each new day as a gift from God and to always be thankful for it.

Fruit of the Mystery: Poverty in Spirit

Our Father

✝

After praying the rosary in the morning with Val for some time, I began thinking of ways to pray for others. I had a list of family and friends whose birthdays I knew of, so I began praying a decade of the rosary for them. I would also text them to let them know that I prayed for them. And, since I am on Facebook, I get notifications of my Facebook friend's birthdays. I would post on their Facebook page that I prayed a decade of the rosary for them. It was a small but sometimes very powerful way to evangelize personally and publicly. I have had responses from some that shared how special it was to be prayed for and I wondered how many times some of these friends had experienced something like that before. As time goes on, and life has its busy and sometimes unpredictable moments, I sometimes miss checking to see who is celebrating a birthday. I try to remember to pray "for anyone celebrating today" to cover my bases. I especially like it when someone's birthday falls on Mondays and Saturdays so that I can pray the third Joyful Mystery, the birth of Jesus, for them.

†

As I was about to turn 50, we were days away from moving into our new home after we had been updating it over the past few months. One Sunday, Val suggested that we take a look at the latest updates of the house after mass. As we walked the 100 or so steps to our soon-to-be new residence, I opened the front door and was surprised by many of our family members! In the middle of painting, staining, and everything else that Val was responsible for, he planned a surprise party for me and pulled it off!

After the singing and hugs, we enjoyed a nice lunch and some wonderful gifts. I had been hinting to Val that I would like a statue of Mary for my birthday to put outside but after seeing the effort he put into the party, I wasn't expecting another gift. The party was a perfect gift. And yet, there was a gift from Val for me to open. It was a beautiful depiction of Our Blessed Mother and

Bernadette, the little girl who saw Mary in Lourdes. I would never have chosen something like this, but leave it to Val to find something so special for me! She sits on our bookshelf in the living room where I can see it often throughout the day.

†

I was scrolling through Facebook one day, and I saw a video of a rosary made out of helium filled balloons floating in the sky. I had never seen such a thing before, and I instantly shared it and commented that I might need to have that floating away after my funeral. After thinking about it for more than a minute, I realized that I wouldn't let any balloons go into the sky because of what it might do to the environment or an animal of some kind, but it was an awesome visual!

†

On September 8, 2018, I wanted to celebrate Mary's birthday in a special way so I placed almost every medal of Mary that I own on a chain to wear to mass that morning. I wore two necklaces with Mary medals on them that were my mom's, and I also created a pair of earrings with tiny miraculous medals that turned out really cute. It was something I had been wanting

to do for a while, and I now have those earrings to wear often, since I love wearing Mary!

✝

On another day of scrolling, I saw a rosary that was made out of cupcakes, and I thought I could have THAT at my funeral luncheon and that wouldn't harm anyone, except someone who may eat too many of them!

✝

Ten Hail Mary's

Chapter 9

The Fourth Joyful Mystery
The Presentation of Jesus in the Temple

And when the time came for their purification according to the Law of Moses, they brought him up to Jerusalem to present him to the Lord. (Luke 2:22)

Dear Mother Mary, please give us the courage to turn to God during the frightful times and present our fears to Him.

Fruit of the Mystery: Obedience

Our Father

✝

My first visit to the Shrine of Our Lady of Good Help in Champion, Wisconsin, was in 2011 with my family. We were spending time in Door County and wanted to make the small pilgrimage to the shrine since I had been hearing a lot about it. This is one of those times when I believe Mary was working on me. I had been going to Adoration and following the pamphlet on how to pray the rosary, but I hadn't memorized it yet. My heart was opening to the rosary, but it was also before the 33 Days retreat when the flood gates opened.

We went down the stairs into the chapel where the room was very dim with lighting but was illuminated with hundreds of candles burning. Blue candles and white candles, large candles and small candles. There were many that were lit and many that were not lit. I stood there for a moment and took it all in. A beautiful statue of Our Lady stood in the front of the room with flowers and candles surrounding her. In front of her was a kneeler. I made my way up to the kneeler and knelt before the statue. It was a double kneeler so two people could venerate her at the same time. I imagine couples or a mother and child kneeling together. I don't remember who knelt with me, but I know someone was beside me since I was on the right side of the kneeler. The reason I mention this is because Mary's head was tilted slightly, and her gaze was directly on me. As I looked up at her, her eyes caught mine and I wasn't able to take my eyes off of her for what seemed like a very long time, but could have only been several seconds. I'm not sure, but I was frozen in time when our gaze met each other's. That was the first time anything like that happened to me. I don't remember any words coming to my heart, but I felt such love from our Blessed Mother. Looking back, I believe that was the moment when my heart was being prepared for whatever life was going to bring me. Even though it would be another two years before I would consecrate myself to Jesus through Mary, it was getting my heart ready for the amazing graces that would fill it.

†

I had never bought a Morning Glory plant before, but when I made my consecration, it was like I was introduced to it for the first time. It's a beautiful clematis with a gorgeous blue flower that is stunning when it's fully open. The name of the plant I bought was actually called "Heavenly Blue", and it was heavenly. Over the years, I have planted the Morning

Glory in a planter behind my small statue of Mary and it has produced wonderful blooms. One day, I stood in front of the ever-growing plant and really took a look at the stages of the Morning Glory. Each stage has a beauty in itself.

Every year, I buy a Morning Glory and one year, my dear friends, DeAnne and Maggie, gave me one for my birthday. I was so excited to plant it in the ground behind my new, bigger statue of Mary that Val gave to me for Mother's Day. As it grew, I realized that it was a different variety of Morning Glory, and I was excited to see what it produced. The flowers were smaller and a deep shade of blue, almost purple, but still so beautiful. As the summer wore on, the plant took on a life of itself. It grabbed on to the tall lily stems that were close by and tangled itself into several other plants and continued to produce flowers that were tucked here and there to create quite a beautiful sight.

†

Ten Hail Mary's

CHAPTER 10

The Fifth Joyful Mystery
The Finding in the Temple

After three days, they found him in the temple, sitting among the teachers, listening to them and asking them questions. (Luke 2:46)

Dear Mother Mary, please help us find Jesus in every situation we encounter and to find the joy in all of the gifts that God has given us.

Fruit of the Mystery: The Joy in Finding Jesus

Our Father

✝

When Val and I pray our morning rosary, we listen to podcasts of the rosary on either the Relevant Radio app or the Laudate app. We pray it without speaking it out loud. When we have more time in the morning, we will listen to the extended version of the rosary with Fr. Rocky on the Relevant Radio app. In it, Fr. Rocky describes what each mystery would have been like if we placed ourselves in the time. He places us IN the rosary. That's what I am trying to accomplish in this book, too.

There are times when I pray the rosary that I am so still or engaged that I don't feel my body. It isn't like I'm actually suspended or anything, but it is a feeling of weightlessness, if that's a word. I move my fingers along each bead, and I hear and feel my stomach gurgling and my breathing is slow and methodical, but other than that, I'm motionless. I like that feeling—or I guess I could say—non-feeling. I wish I could feel that way more often during prayer. I think I've felt that during adoration at times, but mostly during the rosary.

I think of St. John Paul II. He was able to go deep, deep, deep into a place where nothing could distract him during prayer. I would like to be able to do that. I know it isn't easy and it takes a lot of practice and concentration, but it also takes the ability to surrender.

✝

There are so many times during my rosary when revelations come to me. It may be something I've been praying about, an answered prayer that I hadn't realized had been answered, someone who had asked for prayers, or moments with Mary that I should share. It's amazing how the mind works. I am still praying the prayers of the rosary, still placing myself in the mysteries and yet, I am given these moments when things can be so clear to me that were not before.

✝

Have you ever heard that when you hear the sirens of a police car, ambulance, or fire truck, that you can pause and pray a Hail Mary for the safety of all involved? Try it sometime. You never know how Mary can intercede for those who you've prayed for.

✝

Ten Hail Mary's

Chapter 11

Glory be
Fatima Prayer

†

Do you remember the statue of Mary that Ashley bought in Lourdes and gave to me when we were in Rome? Ash bought her because she was pink and when she gave it to me, Mary had changed color to turquoise blue. I thought that was a miracle, or sign of a miracle to come, which it was when my scans came back showing that my cancer was diminishing. I shared that story to hundreds of people, and I continue to tell it to anyone who will listen.

I have an addition to that story. It was May of 2015 and we had recently moved into a small house right next door to our parish. While I was walking past my bedroom one day, I noticed that Mary looked like her blue had faded. As I walked closer, I could barely believe my eyes, she HAD faded to a soft, mint color. I brought her out of the bedroom and set her on our kitchen table. She almost matched the color of our freshly painted kitchen wall. I took a picture of her on my phone and instantly sent a text to Ashley. I was stunned! I didn't know what to think, but it was amazing! I placed Mary back on my nightstand and continued throughout the day, trying to figure out what had happened. I would make a point to look at her throughout the day to see what else might happen. Later that evening, when I was talking about it again to our daughter Sally and Val, I checked her, and she was back to her bright blue again! Of course, I took another picture and sent it to Ashley. That conversation, via texts, was quite filled with exclamation points! Just like this recount of it!!!!!!

What was Mary trying to tell me? I didn't know and I still don't. I just enjoyed knowing that she is so close to me and guiding my days. Mary continues to change colors in no particular pattern, but I have taken pictures of her every time she does. One day, she was almost completely white. It looked like just a coating of glitter was covering the white resin material that she is made of. It was the first day of the 33 Days retreat, and I tried to reason that she was telling me that she will be with our group throughout the retreat. Cool, I thought. I began taking a picture of her next to my clock, so I have a reference as to what time of the day it is. Mary remained white throughout all of the day on Saturday and into Sunday. The longest she stayed a different color. But, after church on Sunday, she was no longer white. The moment that I wondered if it would ever happen, happened. Mary was PINK! She was a soft, baby pink and I took her out to the living room to show Val and it was the first time I was brought to tears over this amazing experience. (I'm tearing up right now.) When Ashley received that picture, she replied that Mary was almost the shade of pink that Ashley remembers her being when she purchased her in December. The words that came to my mind were, "I can't believe this!" But, that's not true. I DO believe it! I don't understand it, but I believe it!

Four hours later, Mary was back to blue again! And, she remained blue for quite some time, although she had been different shades of that blue. I found myself checking in on her so often after that. She is positioned in our bedroom so that I can just glance over my shoulder from our living room, and I can see her looking back at me.

Again, I didn't know what Mary's plan was for me and what she wanted me to do with that experience. I prayed that I could recognize what she placed before me and follow through with what I am supposed to do. It took a while, but I feel that this book is what she wanted me to do. However we can bring people closer to her Son, and if it is going through Mary, I'm all in.

†

Archbishop Emeritus Harry Flynn came to give a talk at our parish, St. Michael's, and he explained that Mary was the best listener.

She listened to Gabriel. She listened to Joseph. She listened in the temple. She listened at Cana. She listened at the foot of the cross.

Archbishop Flynn said we need to be great listeners. It's almost sacramental. We need to listen with our eyes and pay attention.

Am I a good listener? I think I am better at listening to those who are struggling than to those who are not. Not sure why, but probably because I can relate to those who are carrying some kind of cross. Are you a good listener?

After mass, I had the opportunity to talk with the Archbishop and share a few details about my statue of Mary. When he seemed interested in it, I asked him if he would bless the statue for me, which I conveniently brought with me. I also brought along the complete story of how it was given to me in an envelope for him to read later. He was happy to bless my sweet statue.

CHAPTER 12

The Luminous Mysteries

The public life of Our Lord reveals what the reign of God's Kingdom is like – both in the miracles he worked and in his preaching. We meditate on these mysteries asking Our Lady to help us to allow his light to shine in our darkness.

The Luminous mysteries are prayed on Thursdays.

†

As I mentioned earlier, my mom had been praying the rosary all her life, but I didn't know that until she was diagnosed with ovarian cancer in April of 2016. I told her that I wanted to buy her a miraculous medal for her to wear and we got talking about how often she prayed the rosary. I wish I would have asked more questions about why we didn't pray it together as a family or how could it be that I never saw her praying. But we had her current health situation to take care of.

Mom chose a beautiful medal that had a soft teal (the ovarian cancer ribbon color) as the background of Mary on the medal and I bought her a sturdy chain so she could wear it all of the time and not worry about it breaking. I think she

really liked it because I never saw it off unless she was cleaning it.

✝

Mom had a rough go with her chemotherapy after she had an extensive surgery to remove as much cancer as could possibly be taken. It was a long summer for her and dad, with several trips to the hospital when she became dehydrated. Finally, in October, we were all very happy to celebrate mom being done with chemo and her numbers all looked good! She healed from the chemo and spent the winter in Florida with dad.

After a while, mom's labs at her checkups showed there was activity again, so after talking with the doctor and with dad, she decided to try chemo again. It was a different kind of chemo and this time, she didn't lose her hair, but her neuropathy continued to get worse. At times, she couldn't hold a pen in her hands and her feet were cold and she needed to use a cane to steady herself when she walked. But mom never complained.

In January, 2019, mom came home to have surgery on her knee but ended up having surgery to alleviate a bowel obstruction. This was the result of the cancer that was becoming very invasive. Mom couldn't have chemo leading up to the planned knee surgery or after, so she could heal from the surgery. By the time she was able to have chemo again, the cancer had begun to cause more issues. A new chemo was the plan and she started it in early May. She and dad always discussed whether to try another chemo or "let nature take its course" as she would say. We were all optimistic that it would give her more time and accepted whatever she and dad had decided.

Well, that chemo was too strong for mom's body. On Mother's Day when I went to visit her, she was lying in bed, sick and tired. She told me that she was done with chemo if it was going to make her feel that awful. I was sad that it made her feel so bad, but I understood and accepted her decision. I also knew what that decision meant.

The next day, mom was admitted to the hospital for dehydration again and when she was released, we called hospice. At that time, hospice was there to help mom feel better from the one treatment she received. We all hoped that she would "recover" from it and have some quality time left before the cancer would eventually take over. That time was much shorter than we expected.

Mom needed care 24/7 so my siblings and I took shifts to be with her, in addition to the wonderful hospice help that she received. During my overnight shifts, I would sit by mom as she slept and I would pray the rosary, on the birthstone rosary that I gave her.

On Monday, June 24th, at 10:45 pm, my sweet and courageous mom took her last breath and went to meet Jesus. When all of my siblings were gathered at mom and dad's shortly after, I invited whoever wanted to pray the rosary for mom to do so. My sister, Robin, who was with her when she passed, had placed a rosary in mom's hands. As we surrounded her, with her rosaries in our hands, my dear husband led us in praying the Joyful Mysteries. I prayed the rosary using mom's birthstone rosary. That rosary was also lying on the pillow next to mom in her casket. She held the rosary that was a gift from her granddaughter, Kelly, which was the one that Robin placed in her hands when she passed away.

The miraculous medal that I gave to mom early in her diagnosis was around mom's neck as she passed away and in her casket. It now resides around my neck. Mom is always with me.

†

On the morning that mom passed away, I saw that my statue of Mary had changed color a little bit, so I took a picture of it. I posted it on Facebook with the comment, "Mary is quite light today with just a touch of blue in the folds of her mantle. Is this a significant day, Mary?" Of course, it was. Mary was letting me know that she was by mom's side, along with Jesus, getting ready to take her home.

Over the next week, Mary's color continued to change. She was pink, peach, almost white and shades in between. I felt so close to Mary and to mom that week. My favorite color was on the day of mom's funeral. Mary was radiant and I could see so many details in her mantle. Mom was radiant, too.

†

I had a dream about Mary. Of course, many details become vague as I tried to put words to my dream, but I was holding my statue in my hands- telling others about the changing color, when the statue began to change color as I was holding it.

It was like a kaleidoscope as a multitude of colors continued to change, right before my eyes! It was just beautiful! At one time, the statue actually stopped on the colors that are like my statue of Mary and Bernadette. These colors were muted, but still wonderful.

✝

I had a dream about my mom a few weeks after she passed away. She was as beautiful as ever, probably at the age of about 70. She was 80 when she passed, so it was before cancer came into the picture. She had her gorgeous white hair, which I was so blessed to inherit, and her glasses looked like the ones she wore a decade ago. I believe we were in church, and she was sitting next to dad, when she stood up and turned toward me. She smiled really big at me and when I looked at her, the pupils of her eyes were red hearts! Nothing creepy at all about her having red eyes, but a feeling of total happiness and joy! As dreams can go, the scene changed quickly to a kitchen, and she was doing dishes and trying to tell me what heaven was like. I remember her saying in my dream, "It's not like anything I expected!" She continued on with a description of what heaven was like, but I couldn't hear her because there was so much hustle and bustle in the house, just like there always was with a family as big as ours. In my dream, I asked everyone to be quiet so we could hear what mom was saying, but to no avail. I am no expert on dreams, but in my heart that dream told me that mom is in heaven, with our Blessed Mother, and I'm sure they are great friends already. Mary was illuminating me with a message from my mom that night. Thank you, Mary.

CHAPTER 13

The First Luminous Mystery
The Baptism of the Lord

And when Jesus was baptized, he went up immediately from the water, and behold, the heavens were opened and he saw the Spirit of God descending like a dove. (Matthew 4:6)

Dear Mother Mary, help us to open our hearts so we may hear what your Son is asking us to do.

Fruit of the Mystery: Openness to the Holy Spirit

Our Father

✝

Being open to the Holy Spirit has been such a grace for me, although I couldn't identify it as that years ago. It's only by looking back that I can see how that had to be how this journey has played out.

I remember sitting at mass the Sunday after being diagnosed and feeling that God was asking me to share my story. Mary's question, "How can this be?" came to my mind. I wasn't a writer. But I knew I needed to take to prayer what God was asking of me. As it turns out, I AM a writer! My first book was *Mommy's Hats*. It was published in 2009. It's about the year I spent in treatment from my daughter, Sally's point of view. She was only four years old when I was diagnosed. Our other two daughters were ten and twelve, so we needed to explain to them what was going on in simple terms that they would understand. It included actual photos throughout the book. Some pictures of my head being shaved by the girls, receiving chemo, after surgery, but mostly the day-to-day things we dealt with. I found it was a great resource for anyone going through cancer.

After my book was published, I thought I could check that off my list. I believed I had followed God's plan for me, and I went on with life. That lasted for about three years.

I began feeling again, that God wanted to me to share my story and I didn't understand what He was asking of me. I thought I had done just that. Right around that time, my husband, Val, was diagnosed with melanoma and the feeling became stronger that I was to write again, but this time, it was going to be different. I wasn't sure yet, how it was going to be different and with Val's diagnosis, I had plenty to concentrate on besides writing. Thankfully, Val had two surgeries, one that was amazingly miraculous, and he didn't need any further treatment. So, I thought I was supposed to write about how we didn't blame God for Val's cancer or how in the world could God be a just God and let two parents of young children get cancer? I wasn't sure if that was what God wanted me to write about, but we LIVED the truth and shared with others that God IS merciful and loving and that no matter what cross He gives us, we are thankful and continue to praise His Name.

Then, just a few months later came the phone call telling me that my cancer had returned.

I began writing, but not until I prayed to God and asked that He make this all happen. I totally gave it up to Him to guide me to anyone and everyone who I needed to make this come to fruition. I had been journaling for the past few years, so I collected some of those stories that I had written and eventually a theme began to emerge. After several months, I had a publisher and a several more months, I was holding a beautiful book in my hands titled, *Reading Between the Signs*!

What's funny is that even as I was having the second book published, I still didn't consider myself a writer, and at times, I still feel that way. What I do believe is that the Holy Spirit moved me over and over again until I finally admitted that I have been called to write. What's even funnier is that I began writing stories for this book as I was writing stories for the last book!

Am I supposed to write another book? I haven't felt the Holy Spirit tell me that...yet!

†

Ten Hail Mary's

CHAPTER 14

The Second Luminous Mystery
The Wedding Feast at Cana

His mother said to the servants, "Do whatever he tells you." ...Jesus said to them, "Fill the jars with water." And they filled them to the brim. (John 2:5-7)

Dear Mother Mary, let the words you spoke to your Son seep into our hearts so that we may do whatever He tells us.

Fruit of the Mystery: To Jesus Through Mary

Our Father

✝

Fr. Michael Gaitley, who wrote *33 Days to Morning Glory*, wrote that consecrating ourselves to Jesus through Mary is a quick, easy, and secure way to Holiness.

> Mary leads us to Jesus and makes the road to holiness quick and easy, even though she doesn't take away our crosses. In fact, those who are particularly beloved by Mary often have more crosses than others, but Mary makes the crosses sweet and light. (page 45)

When I read those last two sentences during my most recent re-consecration retreat, I stopped in my tracks. I know I've read those words several times already, but they really hit me this time. I believe Mary HAS made my crosses sweet and light, and I really do feel so loved by her.

✝

WINE, Women In the New Evangelization is about empowering women to work within their God-given gifts as women to nurture, heal and build up the body of Christ. When I met Kelly Wahlquist, the founder of WINE, I instantly knew I wanted to be part of this amazing group of women. I invited Kelly to come to my parish and talk to a group of women and invite them to be a part of it, too.

I decorated our parish library with grapes and grapevines and had some wine and cheese. When Kelly saw how I had decorated, she said that she just realized what I could contribute to the team. She pointed out that my gift of decorating would benefit the team at our conferences and events. From that day, I have been blessed to be part of the team and I am honored to decorate for such an amazing group of women. WINE uses the quote, "Do whatever He tells you" as an invitation to follow Jesus.

✝

When our daughter Ashley and her husband Danny, became engaged, we began praying the second decade of the Luminous Mysteries for them and any engaged couples who were preparing for marriage. As there became more couples getting engaged, our list continued to grow.

✝

When my friend, Lisa, turned 50, I wanted to do something special for her, so I decided to pray the Memorare for her for 50 days. I was consistent in journaling at that time so I could keep track of how many Memorares I had prayed and I didn't miss a day!

†

Ten Hail Mary's

CHAPTER 15

The Third Luminous Mystery
Proclaiming the Kingdom

And preach as you go, saying, 'The kingdom of heaven is at hand.' Heal the sick, raise the dead, cleanse lepers, cast out demons. (Matthew 10:7-8)

Dear Mother Mary, help us to be able to have the courage to trust in God at all times.

Fruit of the Mystery: Repentance and Trust in God

Our Father

✝

In 2015, the oncologist that I had been seeing for the last eight years retired. My new doctor scheduled a PET scan to have a starting point with our new relationship. I was excited to see if my prayers were being heard. I had been listening to Relevant Radio, especially at 3:00pm each day to listen to Drew Mariani as he prayed the Divine Mercy Chaplet. So many times over the past several years, I have heard about miracles happening when people prayed the Chaplet. I believed that could happen to me, too. So when it was time to hear of the results of my PET scan, I was ready to hear whatever the results would be. I have always gone into those appointments with the open mind of hearing the news of the cancer being more serious. Not expecting it, but preparing for the possibility of it. I usually don't bring Val along, either, but at that time, I wanted him to meet my new doctor.

When the doctor came in and began by explaining that the results were good and went down the list of results, all were a blur to me because I never focus on that part. She then came to the "Impression" section of the report:

"Stable, no new skeletal lesions." My bones have remained stable for many months, and it was a blessing to hear that they remained that way.

"No soft tissue abnormalities. Overall there is no evidence of active disease."

Wait, what?

"Soft tissue means my stomach, right?" I asked, looking at Val with almost a confused look on my face. Did I hear her correctly?

NO EVIDENCE OF ACTIVE DISEASE ANYWHERE IN MY BODY! ANYWHERE!

As wonderful, absolutely wonderful as the news was, I had a hard time believing what I just heard. MY LIFE WAS SUPPOSED TO BE...that thought made me feel bad, almost like I was lying to Mary when I prayed. There I was, learning from Jesus for years, praying to Him, and serving Him, and now, my prayers were answered and I was questioning Jesus' power to heal me! I know that isn't true! I KNOW how much He loves me, and He showed that by dying on the cross for me and for you!

So, where did I go from there? I had been the face of "living with Stage IV cancer with joy" for the last few years and now what was I? I imagined living with cancer for the rest of my life and I had pretty much accepted the fact that I would probably die of cancer, too. The news was blowing my mind! God was making it very clear that HE was in charge of my life, not me! My special intention for my Prayer to Our

Lady became, "Please show me *how* to honor your son!" I thanked Jesus and His Mother, over and over again, through tears of joy, while shaking my head at times, and I looked forward to seeing which direction they would be leading me!

✝

Having metastatic cancer, there is always the possibility of the cancer moving to other areas of the body. Whenever I have new symptoms, increasing tumor markers, or just time for an updated scan, there's always the chance of a phone call informing me of not so good news. They are never easy to receive, but my trust in God's plan for me and the peace I have in my heart from Mary being by my side through all of this is something I would like others to have.

✝

Ten Hail Mary's

CHAPTER 16

The Fourth Luminous Mystery
The Transfiguration

And as he was praying, the appearance of his countenance was altered, and his clothing became dazzling white. And a voice came out of the cloud, saying, "This is my son, my Chosen, listen to him!" (Luke 9:29, 35)

Dear Mother Mary, help us open our hearts so we may hear what your Son is asking us to do so we may be pleasing to Him.

Fruit of the Mystery: Desire for Holiness

Our Father

✝

My oldest sister, Rita, had a very difficult life. She was diagnosed with Multiple Sclerosis in 1988 and had other health issues for most of her life. In March of 2018, she was diagnosed with cancer in her liver. I remember when I was originally diagnosed, I told Rita that she had to endure so many trials in her life, that I was happy to take on the cancer so that she would not have to. Well, I did my best for 11 years, but I told her I would be by her side, just as Jesus and Mary have been for me, walking with her.

Rita accepted each cross with trust that God knew what He was doing. I have seen strength in her that not many people can exhibit with all of life's difficulties that she has faced. After her diagnosis, she told me that she prays for everybody else and only recently had she begun to pray for herself. How amazing is that?

I was taking Rita to a doctor's appointment. On the way, we were listening to Relevant Radio. The conversation was about Mary, and I asked Rita what her relationship with Mary was like. She was raised Catholic, as I was, but had become Lutheran when she married her husband. She told me that she prayed to Mary and the desire to pray to her had become stronger. She told me that she wanted a statue of Mary and I said I had one that I could give to her. She understood the power of the rosary and was happy to have a statue of the Blessed Mother in her home.

Rita needed surgery in early April of 2019. It was successful, but the surgery put a lot of stress on Rita's body, and she just couldn't recover from it. She spent several days in the ICU. When we realized that she wasn't going to ever come back from it, we needed to accept that her journey home was imminent. I was honored to be in on the conversations with the doctors, along with her two daughters. I asked the girls if it was okay if I asked a priest to come and anoint Rita and they agreed. As we were waiting for the priest to arrive, many family members came to visit Rita—all of her siblings, some of their spouses, nieces, nephews, and her grandchildren. She was conscious some of the time, but mostly asleep.

I had brought in a prayer card of St. Rita of Cascia, the patron saint of the sick, bodily ills, and wounds. I whispered the prayer into Rita's ear as she slept. I prayed it each day I visited her and invited others to pray it for her, as well.

I visited her on Holy Thursday and her two daughters, Holly and Heather, were with her. Rita seemed to be resting comfortably, when suddenly, she would open her eyes and say, "Okay, I'm ready." She did this often, according to the girls and they would just ask her what she was ready for. Sometimes, she would reply, "To go home." We took that as she was ready to meet Jesus and smiled through our tears as we told her she could go home.

I felt moved to sing Amazing Grace to Rita and as I was singing it, she began mouthing the words at different points during the song. It was so beautiful. It took all I had to continue singing without my voice cracking with emotion.

As I was saying goodbye to Rita, I leaned in close to her and told her I loved her, kissed her forehead and that I would see her soon. I asked if she would pray for me when she got to heaven and she replied, "Yes" then puckered her lips for a kiss. I kissed her lips.

As I picked up my drink and was about to leave, she opened her eyes again, saw the drink in my hand and said, "I'm thirsty. What is that?" I answered, "My Diet Coke, would you like some?" A strong "YES" was her reply. Diet Coke was her favorite drink, so I poured a little into a cup. Heather found a small sponge, dipped it into the cup, and placed it in Rita's mouth. She closed her mouth and sucked every drop of that drink. We giggled and asked if she wanted more. She nodded so Heather gave her more. It was such a sweet sight to see Rita so pleased with a few drops of pop.

Rita passed away on the morning of Good Friday. What a day to share with Our Lord! How about the God moment of Rita claiming that she thirsts, just like Jesus on the cross and that she was given something to drink from a sponge.

†

Ten Hail Mary's

CHAPTER 17

The Fifth Luminous Mystery
The Institution of the Eucharist

And he took bread, and when he had given thanks he broke it and gave it to them saying, "This is my body which is given for you. Do this in remembrance of me." And likewise the chalice after supper, saying, "This chalice which is poured out for you is the new covenant in my blood." (Luke 22:19-20)

Dear Mother Mary, help us to understand the graces available to us when we receive your Son in Holy Communion.

Fruit of the Mystery: Adoration

Our Father

✝

Ever since my consecration to Jesus through Mary, I have added a small prayer before I receive communion. We sit in a section of the church that when I look straight ahead of me, the statue of Mary is right there. I love that she is right there for me to pray to her. Right after we pray, "Lord, I am not worthy that you may come under my roof, but only say the word, and my soul shall be healed," I pray the Act of Contrition. Then I take my miraculous medal into my hands and I thank Mary for her fiat, for saying yes so many times in her life. I ask that for her to give me the courage, grace, or whatever I need to be able to give my fiat, too.

✝

It wasn't until I went to a mom's retreat that I learned what adoration was all about. The dads were going to have their retreat the following weekend, so at the end of our weekend, we were asked to sign up for a half hour to pray during the dad's retreat. I admit, I was a little hesitant going into unknown territory, but I signed up. Even after learning about adoration, I still wasn't sure what I was going to do for 30 minutes, but it was nice to sit quietly with Jesus, sometimes praying, sometimes just being. It took me a few more months to finally sign up for an hour on a regular basis. Tuesdays at 1:00pm became my hour and that is where I shared the hour with the family I mentioned earlier and began wanting to learn the rosary.

✝

At some point, I switched my hour of Adoration to Tuesday mornings at 10:00am and that worked really well for me until my most recent switch of chemotherapy. When I needed to switch back to receiving chemo through my port (IV), I needed to be at the Cancer Center for that. For the past few years, I have been blessed to be able to take my chemotherapy orally, at home. My schedule for chemo was two weeks on and one week off. That meant I missed Adoration two weeks in a row, with the third week being able to go. The couple that I shared the hour with was just fine when I wasn't there and happy to see me when I was there. After several months of trying to make that work, I finally decided that I would move my hour to share it with Val on

Thursdays. I hoped that would give me a better chance to make it, even on chemo weeks.

†

In 2015, Pope Francis made a trip to the United States. It was very exciting to watch the coverage on T.V. and at some point, I felt the urge to place my statue of Mary in front of the T.V. What happened as I watched the Pope was pretty cool. Mary changed color right in front of my eyes! The coverage was lengthy from the procession, to the mass, and any  other coverage there was so, I was pretty glued to the television. I pondered what it may have meant why Mary changed colors, but regardless, it was another special experience for me.

†

Ten Hail Mary's

CHAPTER 18

Glory be

Fatima Prayer

✝

I decided that Mary needed a proper place to be honored so I began thinking about a way to create a grotto for her. I shared my ideas with my sisters Renee and Robin and after discussing it for a while, we came up with a pretty neat idea. Renee was creating some cool things by cutting glass bottles. She said she could cut the neck and the base of the bottle off, then cut the body of the bottle in half, buff the edges so they weren't sharp, and that could be the grotto. It worked beautifully! I just needed to come up with a way to make it stand up. That would come later.

When I was shopping for items to make a grotto for my statue of Mary, I found a bag of glass gems that were various shades of blue and thought I could use them to glue on the inside of the grotto to represent the different shades of blue that Mary has been.

The gems were either round or oblong and as I began to sort them into piles of round ones and oblong ones, I saw one piece that wasn't either shape. I looked at it and saw an image that resembles Our Blessed Mother kneeling and

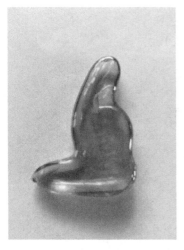

praying. She even looks like she is pregnant. It was and still is quite amazing. I showed it to my extended family and asked what they saw. Some saw Mary immediately and some didn't see her at all, until I pointed her out to them.

I made my grottos, two actually, and saved that special gem to carry with me and share my story with others. Each grotto had a white candle pillar as the base, to elevate Mary. I bought two small, white plates for Mary and the gem-filled half bottle (the grotto) to be set on. I used a hot glue gun to adhere the grotto to the plate. As a final touch, I added a tiny vine with roses on it around the candle pillar and roses at Mary's feet.

I also bought a corner shelf and another piece of art that looks fancy to adhere to the shelf. I hung the shelf in the corner of our bedroom so anyone could see it. I set the grotto and Mary on it.

The second grotto that I made was my traveling grotto. I have given talks on Mary and my journey on several occasions and have used the grotto to place Mary on when I spoke. It gave her a special place of honor. I have also brought along my gem Mary to show the guests. There have been times when Mary actually changed colors as I spoke! The guests were truly amazed!

During a visit to my favorite store, Goodwill, I found a bag of large clear gems. The idea of making copies of my gem Mary, cutting them out, and gluing them to the bottom of the clear gem came to me immediately. I give those out to guests at my talks and to anyone who I feel the Holy Spirit wants me give one to.

The clear gem magnifies the tiny image of Mary, just as Mary magnifies the Lord! The people who received the gem Mary really appreciated having something they could carry with them in their purse or pocket.

CHAPTER 19

The Sorrowful Mysteries

The Passion and death of Our Lord reveal how much God loves us. We meditate on these mysteries asking Our Lady to help us comprehend this love and to experience its life-giving power.

The Sorrowful Mysteries are prayed on Tuesdays and Fridays.

Most days, Val and I will listen to Relevant Radio's podcasts of the rosary but on Tuesdays and Fridays, we listen to a podcast from the Laudate app. There are several different voices to choose from and one day, years ago when I first found the rosary podcasts on Laudate, I came upon a male voice that had an interesting accent. His name is Christian Peschken. His way of praying the Sorrowful Mysteries was unique to me because he added a quick prayer to Our Blessed Mother before beginning the Hail Mary's. I liked them so much so, that I have incorporated my own version of them in this book.

I pictured Christian Peschken as an old and wise man, probably a priest, with a white beard and gentle eyes. When I looked him up to find out a little more about him, I saw a photo of him and was shocked to see he isn't old. Still wise, I'm sure. Not a priest, but a filmmaker. The photo shows him with gray hair and a white beard, so I was spot on in that category! I had to listen to a podcast just to prove this was the same man, though.

Christian converted to Catholicism after watching shows on EWTN.

✝

The Sorrowful Mysteries touch my heart in a way of the suffering part of my journey. I haven't suffered much or often, but there certainly have been some tough days. I've given talks on these mysteries to show others that even in the depth of darkness and despair, Jesus is always with us. We all have crosses to carry, pain to endure, and ultimately, we will all face death. But, if you can focus on the other side of pain and suffering, you will find that you are sanctifying yourself for everlasting life.

When we are in so much pain, we are the closest to Jesus on the cross. We can never feel the amount of pain that Jesus endured, but when we think we can't take any more, think of Jesus and what He did for us. In *33 Days to Morning Glory*, St. Teresa of Calcutta shares how she felt so close to Jesus in her darkest days. She accepted the pain, sorrow and humiliation as a kiss from Jesus.

CHAPTER 20

The First Sorrowful Mystery
The Agony in the Garden

And going a little farther he fell on his face and prayed, "My Father, if it be possible, let this chalice pass from me; nevertheless, not as I will, but as you will." (Matthew 26:39)

Dear Mother Mary, help us to grow closer to your Son by accepting His will for us and help us to be sorry for our sins.

Fruit of the Mystery: Sorrow for Sin

Our Father

✝

On the very first day of my cancer journey, I had several tests done, including an ultrasound of my breast. I can remember as if it was yesterday, lying on the table and the ultrasound technician talking very kindly to me as she was trying to locate the lump I had found. I still wasn't feeling too worried about the situation and so we were just chatting. She finished the ultrasound and told me that the doctor would be in to let me know what she saw on the ultrasound. As the tech walked out the door, all I could think of was "Thy will be done, just give me the strength to get through it." Just as I finished that thought, my doctor walked in, tried to give me a comforting smile and said, "I don't like what I see". Just like that, my attitude changed and so did my life. So, those first four words of my prayer have been my mantra from the very beginning. An amazing grace that I recognized as I looked back on that day was that short prayer that I prayed during a time in my life when I did not have a prayer life. Grace for my heart to open to God to be with me and help me, something that He wants from us every day. That day was the beginning of my relationship with Him, and I will forever be grateful for the grace to accept His invitation.

Even though there are moments that it is hard to accept God's will, I know He has the perfect plan for me. There have been many times that I've gotten emotional while saying the Lord's Prayer, specifically, "thy will be done" especially when I say it out loud at church.

†

Part of the commitment of my consecration to Jesus through Mary, with the *33 Days to Morning Glory* retreat, is to attend the first Saturday mass and go to confession for five months in a row. Since our 2013 consecration, Val and I have been going to mass and reconciliation on the first Saturday of every month with a handful of times that we've not been able to go. Going to confession on a regular basis was not what I did before then but making a commitment to Mary changed everything for me. Going to confession was not a priority for me in the past and when I think of all of the grace I have missed out on for so many years, it makes me sad. But now, I know how powerful cleaning my soul can be and I invite you to be open to receive the grace of confession, too!

As I wait in line for my turn, I pray to Mary and ask her to bring to mind the sins that her Son wants me to confess.

To be honest, I forget some of the sins that I've committed so I need Mary's help to remind me.

✝

In a recent conversation with a friend of mine, I was trying to explain to her what I was feeling about the unpredictability of the cancer that has spread throughout my body. For the past several months, each of my doctor's appointments has been different. Different in the fact that my doctor and I had discussed what the plan would be for the next appointment. When I would have labs, the results of those labs resulted in changing the plan for my chemo treatment that day. At times, it has been unsettling, to say the least. For several years, I have been so blessed to have a chemotherapy treatment prescribed to me and off I went to receive it with such little side effect or issue. It hasn't been that way recently, so it is a new perspective to accept.

As I was talking with my friend, I told her about my original prayer from 2007, "Thy will be done, just give me the strength to get through it". That prayer is just as pertinent as it was in the very beginning, and as simple as it is, it covers a lot of ground.

CHAPTER 21

The Second Sorrowful Mystery
The Scourging at the Pillar

Then (Pilate) released for them Barabbas, and having scourged Jesus, delivered him to be crucified. (Matthew 27:26)

Dear Mother Mary, help us to love others, especially when that love is not returned.

Fruit of the Mystery: Purity

Our Father

†

One of the first shows that I listened to on the Relevant Radio app was the Drew Mariani Show, and more specifically, the Divine Mercy Chaplet that he prayed at 3:00pm every day. I can't remember how I found out about the Chaplet but I'm very thankful for whoever introduced me to it. The Chaplet can be prayed on the rosary beads, but it has different prayers. It was given to us by St. Faustina, who had visions of Jesus describing the prayer to her.

Drew accepts calls from listeners with their prayer requests, so all of the listeners can pray for those intentions along with Drew. There have been specific times that I had just gotten home from an unsettling appointment or just received a phone call with the news of more cancer, when I just lay down on my bed and let Drew's voice as he prayed the chaplet, seep into my heart and give me peace. So many times, callers ask for prayers for someone with cancer and Drew incorporates that personal request but then includes anyone who has cancer to receive the prayers, so it seems that every single day, I am being prayed for through the chaplet. It's quite an amazing feeling. I thought about calling in at times, but never really needed to since I felt covered in prayer already.

The chaplet has had such an influence on me that I wrote about it in my book, *Reading Between the Signs*. When Val and I were planning a trip to the Shrine of Our Lady of Good Help, I wanted to drop off a copy of my book for Drew at the Relevant Radio station in Green Bay since we were going to be so close. Val and I were blessed to be invited to pray the

 chaplet with Drew during our visit! As I mentioned, I don't remember a day that someone with cancer was not prayed for and that day when we prayed with Drew, all five calls were about someone with cancer. Unbelievable? Not with God at the helm!

What was even more special was that when the calls came in about cancer, Drew asked me to respond to the caller. The Holy Spirit took over and words of comfort came out of my mouth.

Since our visit, I have called in for prayers on the day that my mother-in-law and my sister passed away and have gotten through. The chaplet has become quite popular, and many people call in but only five calls are taken most of the time. So, the blessings of getting through to Drew on those days were very special. I was not able to get through on the day that my mom passed away but, someone else called in for a family member who had recently died, and Drew included all of our loved ones who had been called home.

The "Hour of Power" as Drew calls it, has become a part of my day. Sometimes, I will lay down on my bed and listen and sometimes, I fall asleep. But most of the time, I picture myself in the studio with Drew, praying for others with him. My family knows not to text or call between 3:00pm-3:30pm because I won't answer. The alarm on my phone alerts me to get ready to pray the chaplet and unfortunately, there are times when I am unable to stop what I'm doing to pray it. I have been known to be walking in the grocery store with it playing on my phone.

†

In our den, where Val and I spend most of our time and where we pray each morning, we have many pieces of holy art. One specific piece is a candle that we light every morning before we pray. It is a simple, white, pillar candle that we buy at the Dollar Tree store. We buy several at a time. Sometimes, they have a plastic cover that has the image of Our Lady of Guadalupe on it. The candle sits between the nightlight  Mary and a framed image of the Sacred Heart of Jesus.

Every Sunday for the past couple of years, we place the candle in the center of our kitchen table with a small statue of Mary and Joseph next to it. The candle remains lit all day long.

CHAPTER 22

The Third Sorrowful Mystery
The Crowning of Thorns

And they stripped him and put a scarlet robe upon him, and plaiting a crown of thorns they put it on his head, and put a reed in his right hand. (Matthew 27:28-29)

Dear Mother Mary, give us the courage to endure the suffering of our cross and be with us as you were with your Son.

Fruit of the Mystery: Courage

Our Father

†

Val and I planned on spending a night in a Bed and Breakfast in Winona, a town that is a couple of hours away, to celebrate our 23rd wedding anniversary. We also planned on driving down to La Crosse, Wisconsin the next day and visit the Shrine of Our Lady of Guadalupe before heading home. We never got more than a few hours in the B&B. I wasn't feeling well on the drive down but just thought it was my usual digestive issues that show up from time to time. After getting a tour of the mansion, I was really looking forward to lying down for a little bit, but after lying on the beautiful king size bed in our suite for four hours, hoping I would eventually feel better, I finally told Val that we needed to go to the Emergency Room. The pain had gotten worse than I had experienced before.

The pain continued to intensify, and I remembered for the first time, to offer up my suffering. I was actually amazed that I could even think clearly enough to form that thought. I said to Val that I offer up my suffering for…and I began rattling off names left and right. I finished by saying, "and whoever else that hasn't come to my mind." It didn't take any of my pain away, but somehow, it seemed more tolerable.

The doctors in the Emergency Room thought it was kidney stones at first, but it ended up being my appendix. A simple operation, right? Wrong. Being that my body is immune deficient, nothing is simple. I was admitted and Val went back to the B&B for the rest of the night. He was back early in the morning, too early to enjoy the second part of the B-breakfast! After communicating with my doctor at St. Francis, the plan was that I would have a laparoscopic appendectomy and was quickly prepared for it. It was a good thing it was done when it was, because there was a slight perforation in the appendix and if we would have waited any longer, it could have been much more serious.

Once I woke up from my surgery, Val made sure I was in good hands then needed to go home because our youngest daughter, Sally, was home alone. For the next two days, the doctor wanted to make sure I didn't develop any complications from the surgery. It was difficult to be so far away from home and not know any familiar faces. When I began to feel better, I would bring out my Gem Mary, the blue gem that looked like Mary kneeling, and lay it on my white bed sheets. Every nurse that came in got to see it and it would give me an opportunity to talk about Mary with each of them. Some of the nurses couldn't "see" anything and others saw Mary right away. My conversation with those who could see Mary went deeper and it was nice to be able to share our faith with each other.

I was released on a Friday afternoon and Val and Sally escorted me home. I was very sore from the surgery and the over two-hour ride home was a bit uncomfortable but I was happy to be with Val, Sally and Hailey again. The following day was our actual anniversary and also Sally's 14th birthday. Sally, Val and Hailey went to a movie that Sally wanted to see and I actually considered going but chose not to. It was a good thing, because I began feeling icky again. By 8:00pm that night, I was back in the ER, this time at my second home, St. Francis. After hours of tests and labs, I was admitted again.

For the next few days, I was continually checked and observed with the concern of an abscess from my surgery. I had four different doctors in my room at one time. It was crazy and a bit scary at times. As I healed from the four small incisions, other issues would show up and I admit, I had many times when I was really sad. I missed our anniversary, Sally's birthday, and as it turned out, the following day was Father's Day. But, as much as I wanted to see my family, the thought of it exhausted me.

With scheduled follow-up appointments made, I was released into the care of my family and it felt wonderful to sleep in my own bed again. It took a few days before I began to recognize my body and its functions again and that brought me peace. When my mom asked me what she could do for me, my reply was to make that experience a distant memory, and it has become distant for me, but I look back at that time as a difficult hurdle to overcome. It had taken more out of me than some of my cancer surgeries and I had never spent that much time in a hospital at one time.

CHAPTER 23

The Fourth Sorrowful Mystery
The Carrying of the Cross

And when they had mocked him, they stripped him of the robe, and put his own clothes on him, and led him away to crucify him....They came upon a man of Cyrene, Simon by name; this man they compelled to carry his cross. (Matthew 27:31-32)

Dear Mother Mary, as we pick up our cross, we ask that you walk with us and make our cross easier to carry.

Fruit of the Mystery: Patience

Our Father

†

Throughout my cancer journey, I have had many scans, blood tests, etc. and after each one of them, came some time to wait for the results. It is a time to practice patience but also trust in the Lord. In the beginning, waiting was much more difficult than it is now. In the beginning, I didn't have the relationship I have with Jesus and His mother to help me be patient. In the beginning, I counted minutes for that phone call and now, I understand and believe that no amount of time waiting anxiously, will change the outcome of the scan or the lab work that was done, so why worry about it?

There are moments when I wonder what the results may be and I accept that thought, pondering on the possible outcomes. But then I tuck it away in my heart and ask Our Blessed Mother to give me the peace to accept whatever her Son has planned for me. She always comes through. I am able to move on with my day with peace and joy.

When I receive a phone call with the results, and in the past few years, the results have only been blood work to check my tumor markers, I almost forget that a phone call is coming but as soon as I see "Cancer Center" pop up on my caller ID, I know what's coming. It doesn't take my breath away or give me any anxious feelings.

I instantly know that Mary is covering me with her mantle, and everything will be okay.

In the past several months, those phone calls have been informing me that my tumor markers have gone up. My tumor markers should be 35 or below and they had been in the normal range for quite some time until January of 2019, when they popped just above the normal range. Because it was just a few points, we weren't concerned but we definitely kept our attention on it at my next appointment. In February, they went up another four points, the next month they jumped 30 points, then 100 points the following month. It was at that point that we made the change to a new chemotherapy for me.

Starting a new chemotherapy is a little unsettling because there are new side effects to look out for and the wonder of if/when they will arrive. I try not to schedule too many things on days after I receive treatment in case I don't feel well. That gets a little old having to do that every week, and it's really difficult to try to plan anything a month or more out on the calendar. That's where patience comes in again and again and again.

CHAPTER 24

The Fifth Sorrowful Mystery
The Crucifixion

And Jesus cried again with a loud voice and yielded up his spirit. And behold, the curtain of the temple was torn in two, from top to bottom; and the earth shook, and the rocks were split. (Matthew 27: 50-51)

Dear Mother Mary, help us to focus on the joy of heaven when we are close to being called home.

Fruit of the Mystery: Perseverance

Our Father

✝

I woke up one Father's Day, not feeling well, which surprised me. Most of the time, I wake up feeling well rested and good to go, even if I went to bed feeling not so great. The first thing I do once I'm awake is to pray a Hail Mary. Sometimes, I pray another Marian prayer, but most of the time, it's a Hail Mary. After I pray, I evaluate how I'm feeling and wonder what God has planned for me for the day. I may run down the list of what *I* think the day will be like. Sometimes, God's plan and mine mesh well together. Sometimes God has different plans for me. That's what He did on that Father's Day. My plan was to make Val a nice breakfast, go to mass and then celebrate with Val's side of the family in the afternoon. Unfortunately, none of that happened for me.

I felt awful, both physically and emotionally. Physically, my stomach was in knots, more like my intestines were in knots and the pain was pretty constant. Emotionally, my heart hurt that it was Val's special day, and I couldn't make him breakfast, let alone sit next to him at mass and ultimately, not be able to celebrate with him and his family. Val has always been so generous with his love, his time, and his responsibility as a husband and father. Now, in recent years, his support as my caregiver, he has been extraordinary. That's why it bothered me that I wasn't able to show my appreciation for all he has done for me. Of course, he said it said it was okay, because he doesn't think about himself, but I still felt bad. At least I was able to convince him to go and celebrate with his family.

I spent the day in bed. That alone gives you an idea of how bad I felt. I would rather be on my favorite chair during the day, maybe watching TV or a movie, but not that day. I opened the Relevant Radio app on my phone and listened to the shows that were playing. After a while, I couldn't even listen to that anymore. I was in so much pain that all I could do was to pray Hail Mary's over and over again. As I lay doubled up on my bed, in the bathroom and every step in between. I must have prayed hundreds of them. Finally, hours later, I found relief and I was very grateful to Mary.

✝

Fr. Rocky, the CEO of Relevant Radio, has the gentlest voice and it's his voice that I hear daily when Val and I pray the rosary. The app offers many things, and the rosary is what we use the most, besides me just listening to the live shows throughout the day.

A couple of years ago, I was blessed to meet Fr. Rocky at a Relevant Radio banquet in the Twin Cities. I told him how much I appreciate his voice and that when I'm feeling awful, it is his voice that brings me comfort.

CHAPTER 25

Glory be

Fatima Prayer

†

The following is from my journal dated December 8, 2015:

When I woke up this morning, I glanced over at Mary, which is what I do every morning. I could see, even in the darkness, that Mary was not blue. I turned on the lamp and there she was, pink as ever! I took another picture as I smiled and silently thanked her for this beautiful gift. I went out to the living room and prayed my rosary and I felt the urge to check on Mary, once the rosary was done. Guess what? She was blue again! I took another picture, and my smile was even bigger than it was when I first woke up. Not only was SHE pink and then blue, the morning sky was both pink and blue! So many gifts I was given this morning! When I told my mom about it, she told me that Fish Lake, the lake where I grew up, was even pink!

So, here we are. On this Feast of the Immaculate Conception of the Virgin Mary, I feel I am supposed to write about Mary. For what purpose? That, I do not yet know. I pray daily that I am able to say "yes" to whatever I am asked to do, just like our Blessed Mother did, with grace and with a joyful heart.

I have been so blessed and I want to give thanks for the blessings and the mercy that God has given me. I want to continue to tell my "Mary story" to anyone who will listen, and I hope by doing so, others may be filled with the love and joy from our Blessed Mother.

✝

The story gets better! I thought it was pretty amazing what happened on the one year anniversary of Ashley buying the statue for me but I could not have imagined what would happen the next day. When I woke up, I didn't expect to see that Mary was pink again but was quite tickled that she was. Again, I took a picture and again, I went to pray the rosary. And, again, went to see what color she was after and she was blue again!!!

I know, right?

The amazement didn't stop there either. Mary was pink, then blue again the next three days! That would make it five days in a row that she was pink when I woke up then blue when I was done praying. The fifth day was December 12th, which is the feast of Our Lady of Guadalupe. Two feast days within five days of each other, pretty special. My statue changing colors for those five days, priceless.

I can't wait to meet Mary in heaven and ask her about the significance of her changing colors, especially on these five days. The statue has never done anything like that before or since, which makes it even more special to me and more powerful to others when I tell them about it.

CHAPTER 26

The Glorious Mysteries

In triumph, Our Lord empowers us to follow him courageously. We meditate on these mysteries asking Our Lady to intercede for us, that we may always keep in mind the glory of God as we see to do his will here on earth.

The Glorious Mysteries are prayed on Wednesday's and Sunday's.

✝

A few years ago, my health wasn't very good, and I pondered in my heart, as Mary often did, many things. One of those things was if I would live to see any grandchildren. We were blessed with a beautiful granddaughter, Lucy Marie, in May of 2018. I was over the moon in love with her and when Val asked me one day what I thought about being Lucy's daycare, I jumped at the idea! He shared that since we don't know what direction my health would take at any moment, we should take advantage of the opportunity to spend as much time with Lucy as we can. Val said he would be available to help at any time and he suggested I bring the idea to adoration and pray about it. I told him I didn't need to pray about it at all, I was in!

Lucy came in August when our daughter, Ashley went back to work. On the Friday of that first week, as I helped Ashley get Lucy's car seat into the car and say goodbye for the weekend, I began to get emotional. I finally understood what it meant to love a grandbaby more than one can imagine. That love has grown deeper and deeper and every day that I have Lucy, I am blessed.

Something that I have with Lucy that I didn't have with my three daughters is my deep and growing faith, especially my relationship with our Blessed Mother. One of the first things that Lucy did that made my heart swell was her holding my miraculous medal in her tiny hands as I rocked her to sleep. Once she began reaching for things, she would always go after my medal and I would tell her that it was Mary. When the stage of everything going into her mouth started, there went Mary into her mouth! I would gently take the medal out of her mouth and encourage Lucy to give Mary a kiss. I would show her how to kiss Mary and sometimes, I would have to actually take off my necklace when she was infatuated with it.

In our den, where Lucy slept, is a night light Mary. It is the bust of Mary that is all white so the light shines through her beautifully. She is looking down onto the flower petals that are resting in her hands. Her blue mantel is covering her head and shoulders that is a separate piece. It has its cord with an *off* and *on* switch. I have never turned off the night light and amazingly, the small light bulb stayed lit for much longer than a normal light bulb and it wasn't a halogen or long-life light bulb. I guess Mary really wanted to light the room for us! She is on a shelf, and she can even be seen by passersby outside. I often wonder what they think when they see Mary glowing in our house. The first time I saw it lit from outside, I was tickled to think that our Catholic faith was seen not only when guests come into our home and see all of our faith items displayed, but for everyone who takes a glance at our house as they walk by.

When it is time for a nap, I bring Lucy into our den, and we say hello to Mary and Jesus. There is a framed image of Jesus that sits right next to the night light Mary. It has become a routine and now, when I say, "Let's say good morning to Mary," she looks right at her. She blows her a kiss and I ask that Mary watches over Lucy while she sleeps.

I believe that Lucy definitely knows that Mary is very special, and she knows the different kinds of Mary's that I have in our home: statues, pictures, books, medals, and even on my t-shirts. It is such an honor to expose Mary and her Son to Lucy in every way so that she develops a love for them and  even though she may not remember these early years with Grandma, the foundation has been placed in her heart.

✝

When Lucy first came to my house, I enjoyed rocking her to sleep and sometimes, I held her through her entire nap. Who am I kidding, I did that a lot, and I still do that sometimes! One particular time, she got a hold of my miraculous medal and didn't let go of it even after she fell asleep. What a beautiful thought that Lucy knew exactly what she was doing when she took hold of our Heavenly Momma!

†

Lucy came really early in the morning and sometimes, Val and I hadn't had time to pray our rosary so Lucy would join us. She would watch us slide our hands along the beads and I believe she was mimicking us, except for the part when she put the rosary in her mouth.

†

Okay, you can probably tell that I took just a few photos of Lucy during her time at Grandma's but each and every one of them were so special, especially when it included telling her about Our Blessed Mother and how much she loves Lucy. In the photo below, Lucy matched the color that Mary was that day and I wanted to see what Lucy thought of the statue. Of course, she wanted to put Mary in her mouth, but I would make the sound of a big kiss and tell her that she was giving Mary a kiss.

Chapter 27

The First Glorious Mystery
The Resurrection

Then the other disciple, who reached the tomb first, also went in, and he saw and believed; for as yet they did not know the Scripture, that he must rise from the dead. (John 20:8-9)

Dear Mother Mary, help us to have faith in you and your Son to be able to feel your presence throughout the day.

Fruit of the Mystery: Faith

Our Father

✝

One Easter Monday morning, I happened to look out my kitchen window that faces the back parking lot of our church. At the back side of the parking lot is a small shed that holds tools and small equipment for the church. On this morning, though, there was something that looked quite interesting that caught my eye. I looked and even squinted my eyes to try to see it clearer since it was so far away. My first thought was, "Why is Mary standing outside?" It looked like Mary was standing in front of the shed! I grabbed my binoculars to get a close-up look. It was a bag of salt! It was a white bag with blue on it. Some of the salt was used from the bag so it was thinner and it resembled the slender image of Our Blessed Mother.

I took a picture of it on my phone and posted it on Facebook, one of my favorite ways to evangelize, to see what others saw. The comments were fun to read. Some could see how the bag of salt looked like Mary. My close friends really got a kick out of it because they know all about my statue and its changing colors. That post received a lot of likes that day.

✝

In honor of the one-year anniversary of receiving Mary, I created a snow Mary! Can you see the resemblance? I even made a rosary in the snow, too!

We live across the street from our catholic school and while I was building the Mary in the snow, kids were shouting from the playground, asking what I was building. When I was almost finished with the rosary, a kindergarten class, with their teacher, walked across the street and I asked them if they knew what kind of snowman I made and what all of the little mounds of colored snow were. It took a little bit of hinting to help them but once they were told it was Mary and the rosary, they thought it looked really cool. I told them that when they were at school and looked over to the snowman, that they could say hello to Mary.

✝

On December 31st 2018, Val looked out the window and asked me why there was a statue of Mary sitting outside and up against the school. I walked to our big picture window and smiled when I saw what looked like a statue of Mary. We went back and forth about why it would be outside in the harsh weather conditions and why would it be placed there. I finally decided that I needed to investigate. I bundled up and took my phone with me. I took a few photos from our first perspective and then I began recording my investigation as I walked toward the school. As I got closer to the ice image, I could see it more clearly. Surprised, yet not surprised, there was a downspout with a clump of frozen ice that created what looked like the Virgin Mary, but only from a distance. Once I got close, it just looked like a chunk of ice. I love when Mary does things like this. And, I really love that it was Val who saw it first!

✝

When my mom needed surgery for cancer, I brought a bottle of Holy Water from Lourdes and my little Gem Mary with me to the hospital. While she was waiting to go into surgery, I was able to bless mom with the Holy Water and showed her the Gem Mary to let her know that Mary would be with her in surgery. Two of my sisters were with us and so was my dad. When I was showing mom my Gem Mary, dad asked me what it was. I showed him and told him the story behind it, and he commented that I would see Mary in a piece of toast. I took that as a great compliment! Dad understands how important Mary is to me, even though he may not feel the same way. That makes my heart swell with even more love for him.

✝

Ten Hail Mary's

CHAPTER 28

The Second Glorious Mystery
The Ascension

*So then the Lord Jesus, after he had spoken to them, was taken up into heaven,
and sat down at the right hand of God. (Mark 16:19)*

Dear Mother Mary, help us to have the hope of eternal life with
your Son.

Fruit of the Mystery: Hope

Our Father

†

Val and I made another pilgrimage to Our Lady of Good Help
to celebrate our anniversary in July of 2018, in conjunction
with a visit to Door County, where we spent our Honeymoon
25 years earlier.

Val and I wanted to go to confession and attend mass at
the Shrine, so we got there early enough to go down into the
chapel and venerate Mary and just sit in her presence before
we headed upstairs to get in line for reconciliation. The line
had a good dozen people in it, and it gave us time to enjoy
the beauty of the church and to prepare ourselves for
confession. I have mentioned that regular confession has

been such a grace for me. In my mind, receiving absolution at the Shrine was going to be filled with more grace.

When I was just a few people away from entering the confessional, I began thinking of past sins that I have already confessed and been forgiven for and wondered why they were coming to my heart again. Soon, I was kneeling behind the screen and asking for forgiveness for those past sins again. Without getting into private details, it was the best confession I had ever had, and I am truly grateful for Mary bringing those old sins to mind to create the complete cleansing of my soul.

†

At every visit to the Shrine, I like to go to the gift shop and purchase something special for our family. One thing I was particularly looking for was a rosary with large beads for my mom. She had developed neuropathy from chemotherapy, and it was difficult for her to hold onto the small beads of her rosary. I found one that was a decade, made of brown beads and a wooden cross. I couldn't wait to give it to mom. I bought some small wooden crosses for each of the kids and Val and I each bought a t-shirt with Our Lady on it.

†

In 2019, Val and I made a special pilgrimage to the Shrine, this time it was for the annual Walk to Mary. When I met Fr. Rocky at the Relevant Radio banquet, he asked me if we were going to the walk that year. I told him I wasn't able to, and he said, "Maybe next year." And, so it happened. I was really excited to be part of the walk but wasn't sure how much walking I could actually do due to my health at that time. It really didn't matter the amount to steps I took, but the desire to be close to others who loved Our Blessed Mother, too.

I really wanted to go to the Shrine, and we thought it was best to do it before the thousands of people got there. I had brought along with me a list of special intentions that I wanted to light candles for so that's where we went first. Being down in the chapel and kneeling before Mary is such a special time for me. I sat in front of her and wrote out cards to each of the people I prayed for and lit a candle for.

✝

After, we went to the gift shop, of course, and I found small plastic figures of Jesus and Mary to give to Lucy and I found another big, beaded rosary for my mom. The day before we planned to leave for the Shrine, my mom called and asked if I would buy another rosary for her because she took the one I gave her to Florida and it was still there. I was happy to buy another one for her. Little did I know that my mom  would pass away the following month and I would have that rosary lying at the feet of my statue of Mary.

✝

We went to one of the stops along the walk where the pilgrims would have lunch. We signed up for lunch and we thought we would have a chance to meet some of the pilgrims while

enjoying lunch together, which we did. There was a couple standing outside the building where lunch was going to be served and we introduced ourselves and then asked them where they got their t-shirts. Since Val and I didn't make it to the beginning of the walk, we didn't have a chance to buy one. Right after the couple told us that we could order a shirt online, a truck pulls up right next to us with boxes of shirts to sell! Thank you, Mary! We each bought one and were blessed that they had our sizes because there were only a few left. We had a lovely visit with the couple during lunch and after, they continued on their trek, while Val and I headed back to the hotel.

The following day, we went back to the Shrine to celebrate mass with Fr. Rocky. Then, Fr. Rocky led everyone around the edge of the shrine as we all prayed the rosary. It was just what I was hoping for, to be among others who loved and adored Mary. When everything was over, I had the opportunity to have my picture taken with Fr. Rocky and just a moment to visit with him.

✝

There was a day, a couple of cycles into my new chemo that I felt really sick, and I was not in a good place. I asked Val to pray the rosary with me while I was lying in bed. I reached for mom's large decade rosary and held it tight as I prayed. Tears rolled down my face as I prayed and before the rosary was over, I physically felt better. I thanked my heavenly mother and my earthly mother for helping me feel better.

†

Ten Hail Mary's

CHAPTER 29

The Third Glorious Mystery
The Descent of the Holy Spirit

And there appeared to them tongues as of fire, distributed and resting on each one of them. And they were all filled with the Holy Spirit and began to speak in other tongues. (Acts 2:3-4)

Dear Mother Mary, help us to be open to the Holy Spirit so that we may share our love of God with others.

Fruit of the Mystery: Love of God

Our Father

†

Each year when graduation parties are about to begin, I always try to think of something special to give the graduates other than cash. Cash is always good, but I want to give them something to help grow their faith as they head off to college.

One of my better ideas is that in the card that I give the graduates, I tell them that Val and I will pray for them every Sunday when we pray the third decade of the Glorious Mysteries, the descent of the Holy Spirit. Having been confirmed just two years prior, I thought it would be good to remind them that they are filled with the Holy Spirit, and they have been called to let the Spirit work through them. I hope that by those young adults knowing that we are praying for them every Sunday, they will feel those prayers, especially when they are in need of them. Who knows, it may encourage them to find a friend, find a group, or find a church to help them continue to grow in their faith, wherever they are. I also slip in some cash and a rosary decal.

†

With my statue of Mary changing colors so often at times, I occasionally will receive a text from a friend asking me what color Mary is on any given day. I will reply with a photo of her at that moment and a smiley emoji. Also, many times when I look at my phone, it is charged to 33%!

†

Ten Hail Mary's

Chapter 30

The Fourth Glorious Mystery
The Assumption of Mary

For since we believe that Jesus died and rose again, even so, through Jesus, God will bring with him those who have fallen asleep. (1Thessalonians 4:14)

Dear Mother Mary, give us the grace to surrender to your Son's love and mercy at the time of our death.

Fruit of the Mystery: Grace of a Happy Death

Our Father

†

With the likelihood of me passing away from cancer, there have been different times along my journey when I have really given a lot of thought to what I want my funeral to be like. I began writing some of my wishes down and every once in a while, I will go back and change something here or there. Those changes usually show the growth in my faith to focus on others that will be at the funeral instead of the focus being on me. Of course, there is no way to take the focus OFF of me, but many of my wishes are to help those that are still here to cope, accept, trust, believe, that my journey has been a great one.

†

One of the wishes I have is to give away my rosaries to my siblings. In my family, there are different levels of faith, and I think we all do a pretty good job at respecting those levels. I am the most vocal and visual about my faith, and I appreciate my siblings allowing me to express my faith as much as I do. I'm sure there are siblings that don't know how to pray the rosary, just as I didn't know how to, but my hope is, that my siblings will pray a rosary when they have received news that I have passed away. I don't know if any of them would be with me as I take my last breath, but from wherever they are, I would love for them to offer that one last act of love for me and pray the rosary.

†

My mother-in-law, Loretta, loved the rosary and prayed it often. It was her mother who I wrote about praying rosaries for the kids, grandkids, etc. and wrote down which mystery, the date, and the time she prayed it. She passed on to her children the great devotion to Our Lady and Loretta passed it on to her children, as well.

When Loretta was in hospice at home, there were many family members caring for her every need. One night, Grandpa Val (Val's dad) needed our help, so my Val and I went over to their house. While Grandpa Val was being cared for, I was sitting with Loretta. She slept most of the night and early in the morning, when she woke up, I asked her if she would like to pray the rosary with me. I went into her bedroom—her hospice bed was in the living room—and saw her large collection of rosaries hanging on her dresser post. I looked for the birthstone rosary that I had given but couldn't see it at a quick glance, so I took the first blue one I found. I opened my Relevant Radio App and turned on Fr.

Rocky's voice and we prayed together. Her eyes were closed and she didn't move her fingers across the beads but that didn't matter. She was engulfed in the love of Mary as she lay on her bed. That moment will remain deep in my heart because that was the last time I was alone with Loretta before she passed away.

Every time I would say goodbye to Loretta, I would kiss her forehead, tell her I loved her and that I would see her soon. The first time I did that, I got quite emotional because I also thanked her for loving me so much and making me feel so special in her family. I apologized for crying and she said in a soft voice, "That's okay."

When Loretta passed away in the early morning of February 4th, her family gathered around her and prayed a rosary to send her off to heaven. Somewhere I had seen that the roses that were on Mary's feet were yellow, so I took the small yellow roses from one of Loretta's bouquets from her funeral and placed them near Mary's feet, along with the mint green rosary that  Loretta had recently given me. Those roses have dried nicely and remain at the feet of my statue.

✝

Since my mom, my sister, and Loretta's passing, I pray for them on this particular decade. I know they did not assume into heaven like Mary did, but I like to imagine them in heaven as I pray for them. I believe they each experienced the grace of a happy death. I also pray that I may experience that same grace someday.

✝

I received a text from Val one day and he told me that there are 33 steps from his mom's grave to my mom's grave. I replied, "Of course, there are!"

†

Ten Hail Mary's

CHAPTER 31

The Fifth Glorious Mystery
The Coronation

And a great sign appeared in heaven, a woman clothed with the sun, with the moon under her feet, and on her head a crown of twelve stars. (Revelation 12:1)

Dear Mother Mary, help us to come to you to intercede for us.

Fruit of the Mystery: Trust in Mary's Intercession

Our Father

✝

At the annual mom's retreat at my parish, we began the evening in the main sanctuary. Father Jim graciously joined us for adoration. He processed in, holding the Monstrance with his covered hands, in respect for the holiness of Jesus' Presence before him. He placed Jesus on the altar and proceeded to read us the story of the woman who had been inflicted by continuous hemorrhaging for 12 years.

I was sitting in the pews, directly in front of Jesus and for a while, I couldn't take my eyes off of Jesus. Then, tears began to fill my eyes as I was basking in His love and mercy. For several minutes I continued to allow my tears to slowly travel down my cheek as I smiled.

In 2015, as table leaders, we were asked to model what to do during adoration on Friday night, in case there were women there for the first time, just like I was six years prior. Again, the story about the faithful woman, wanting to just touch the hem of Jesus' clothes was read. It is a powerful story for the mothers to hear because, we know, we all have areas in our lives that could use some healing. I was the first to walk up to the monstrance and kneel before Jesus. The altar table had been dressed with the beautiful gold monstrance and a simple white cloth that gently wrapped the stand of the monstrance. The white cloth represented Jesus' tunic. I knelt close to the altar so that I could touch the cloth. I held it in my hand as I looked up at Jesus. Time stood still. As my eyes were fixed on Jesus, I heard the words in my heart, "Rhonda, let me heal you." I placed my face into the white cloth and began to cry softly.

Up until that point on my cancer journey, believe it or not, I did not pray to be healed from cancer. Call me crazy, but I thought my mission in life was to serve God by serving others on their journey with a cross, specifically cancer, by being an example of how joyful life can be, living with Stage IV cancer. Don't get me wrong, I prayed for good test results. I prayed for pain to go away. I prayed that tumor markers would go down. But, ultimately, I prayed for acceptance of God's will.

That night in the sanctuary, kneeling before Christ, I accepted his offer. I did not know exactly what that meant but my heart had opened to being healed.

†

The following day of the mom's retreat, we were led upstairs to the main sanctuary again and as we entered, I could see many unlit candles on the altar. Some were blue and some were white. There was also a large, framed image of Our Lady in the middle of the altar. The candles were in the shape of the rosary, with the blue candles representing the ten Hail Mary's and the white candle representing the Our Father's. A candle was lit with each prayer we said. The glow of the rosary began to take shape. It was gorgeous once it was lit. The first time I saw it, tears came to my eyes. Each year after that, the same thing happened. I looked forward to that rosary. I'm sure it was as powerful to others as it was to me.

†

I rarely take off my miraculous medal, and one day, while I was changing the medals, I realized that the figure of Mary on the medal I was wearing had a tinge of pink on it. I understand that the silver may be wearing off of the medal, but it was still quite interesting that the changing of the color of Mary happens to fit right into my little world.

†

Ten Hail Mary's

CHAPTER 32

Glory be

Fatima Prayer

†

I heard on Relevant Radio about ways to honor Mary during the month of May. One way that sounded fun was to place a flower at her feet each day and by the end of the month, a beautiful bouquet would be created. I decided to try it, so I went searching for tiny flowers to compliment her small statue. I found almost the same color roses that I used for her grotto. I also bought some blue flowers that I would place at her feet on special days in May, such as my birthday, Mother's Day, the day I was diagnosed, and Ashley's birthday. (Lucy wasn't born yet, but she would have gotten a very special flower on her birthday!)

I decided to take a picture of each day with the newly added flower at her feet and post it on Facebook- stating the special day that it may have been and showing my followers what color Mary was that day. Even though there wasn't a drastic change in Mary's color, there were certainly days that she was a different color. My Facebook friends noticed and commented on her change. They posted comments of amazement, wonder, and awe.

It would have been really special if Mary would have changed more dramatically, but that isn't how she works.

She is humble in her works and subtle in her drawing us closer to her and her Son.

✝

On one of my many trips to Goodwill, I was looking through the short sleeve shirt section with nothing particular in mind. I came upon a t-shirt that looked like shades of green tie dye. I only saw the shoulder and collar, mind you, because it was

tucked in with many shirts. It caught my eye, and I took it off the rack. What I saw when I lifted it from the rack made me smile. The entire front of the shirt was the face of Mary! I had never seen anything like that before and how was it that that particular shirt caught my eye? Of course, I bought it and I wear it with such admiration of Mary.

That's not the only t-shirt I own with Mary's image on the front of it. Do you remember the shirts I bought on two visits to the Shrine? I guess I have a collection of Marian t-shirts, without even trying. During the month of May, I tried to wear a Mary shirt every day in honor of her. I can get away with only having three since I'm home a lot and can wear the same shirt more than once. I missed a few days, so I guess I need to find more shirts.

✝

Along with wearing shirts with Mary on it, I also like to honor Mary on her feast days by wearing something blue. I have several pieces of clothing that I wear for those special occasions and also when I give talks. I like to think that my blue is Mary's mantle, covering me with her love.

✝

Another year during the month of May, I wanted to honor Mary each day on Facebook. I knew that I had many Marian prayer cards so I gathered them together and discovered that I had enough to post one for each of the 31 days in May. I chose special ones for the special days and took photos of the front of the card with its image of Mary, and I also took a photo of the prayer on the back of the card. The only time I posted any comments when I posted the prayer card was when it was a feast day or a special day. Otherwise, I just posted the prayer card. It was very interesting to see how many likes and comments I received throughout the month. Such a simple way to evangelize, and possibly introduce Mary to someone who didn't have a relationship with her.

CHAPTER 33

Hail Holy Queen:
Hail, Holy Queen, Mother of Mercy. Our life, our sweetness and our hope. To thee do we cry, poor banished children of Eve. To thee do we send up our sighs, mourning and weeping in this valley of tears. Turn, then, most gracious advocate, thine eyes of mercy towards us; and after this, our exile, show unto us the blessed fruit of thy womb, Jesus. O clement, O loving, O sweet Virgin Mary.

Pray for us, O Holy Mother of God, that we may be made worthy of the promises of Christ.

Let us pray...
O God, whose only begotten Son, by His life, death, and resurrection, has purchased for us the rewards of eternal life. Grant, we beseech Thee, that by meditating on these mysteries, of the most holy rosary of the Blessed Virgin Mary, we may imitate what they contain and obtain what they promise, through the same Christ our Lord. Amen.

Sign of the Cross.

†

I made a Cursillo weekend in 2009, during the time when my faith was being catapulted to the next level and it, too, made a big impact on my relationship with Jesus. The weekend is four days long. You eat, sleep and worship at the location with no contact with the outside world. It was glorious. The women go one weekend and the men go another weekend so if there are children, there is a parent to take care of them. There is adoration, mass, reconciliation, talks, discussions and so much more.

After the weekend, you begin to meet with others on a regular basis who have made a weekend. Most of the time, it is weekly. These small groups become like family to you because it is where you are able to share your faith, which sometimes includes some struggles and hopefully, many steps closer to Christ.

Once you attend a Cursillo weekend, you are able to work a weekend, which I was blessed to do. My dear friend, Nancy, was the leader for the weekend and there were several times throughout the weekend when we prayed the rosary. By that time, I had been learning the mysteries of the rosary but still would not have been able to lead it without reading from a pamphlet. There were also a few extra prayers that I was still trying to learn by heart. One of them was the prayer that comes after the Hail Holy Queen. The part that begins with, "Let us pray..." I feel that after praying it several times that weekend, I was able to remember it from then on.

AFTERWORD

A Happy and Beautiful Death

Rhonda prayed for a happy death. She wanted to be surrounded by family and have them pray for her to meet Jesus face to face.

And that's exactly what happened.

Rhonda's diagnosis of cancer in 2007 did not bring her down. In fact, those who know her best would tell you it seemed to lift her up. How is this possible? By faith. Her faith grew as she trusted in the Lord. When her cancer was in remission, she helped to reach out to others with cancer through the Pink Prayer Warriors Ministry, which she helped start.

When her cancer returned in 2013, her faith continued to increase. She found an advocate in our Blessed Mother. Rhonda turned to Mary's intercession and found you can still live with joy despite having Stage IV cancer.

Most of us will not be given time to prepare for our death like Rhonda. Yet should we not all prepare for it? Our goal as a family was Heaven. Once we figured that out, we were able to LIVE. Fear steals our ability to live.

Rhonda and I were blessed with 27 years, 10 months, and 10 days of marriage. We had our good times and bad, and of course, sickness and health. The fruits of our marriage were our three beautiful daughters: Ashley, Hailey, and Sally; our two sons-in-law: Danny and Alex; and our three grandchildren: Lucy, Oliver, and Clare.

As a family, we celebrated birthdays, baptisms, first communions, confirmations, weddings, and much more including Holy Days. Rhonda's last mass she attended was Easter Sunday on April 4th, 2021. We had a wonderful celebration after mass to give thanks to our Lord for his passion, death, and resurrection.

By the end of the week, Rhonda was in the hospital. There we found out her cancer was on the move again, this time to her brain. Many family members and friends had once again reached out to support Rhonda and our family.

God gives us many graces, most of which we don't really see. On the afternoon of April 28th, Rhonda's time on this earth was coming to a close. She experienced a cardiac arrest. When the doctor told me "There's nothing we can do. You need to call your family," my heart sank. Even though I knew something like this could happen, I was not prepared for that moment when it did happen. But God was with me.

The hospital administrator asked what I needed. "A Catholic priest," I said. The priest on duty at Methodist Hospital quickly got to the ICU to anoint Rhonda while I started to call family from another room.

When I went into the ICU, Rhonda was breathing peacefully with a ventilator. My beautiful wife was now in her final hours. We had talked about how she wanted to be surrounded by family praying her to heaven.

With my daughters present, along with Rhonda's sisters, we turned on the live broadcast of the Divine Mercy Chaplet with Drew Mariani on Relevant Radio. The Hour of Power starts at 3:00pm, a prayer Rhonda listened to daily.

After the Chaplet, Rhonda's wish was for the family to pray the rosary, which we did. I was surprised I had the strength to lead it.

Rhonda continued to breathe peacefully without a ventilator. She was so quiet; it was like watching a newborn baby sleeping.

After the rosary, we sang a few hymns. Then each of us said our final goodbye's. When it was my turn, I grabbed her hand. I told her we are all going to be okay. Then I told her to go ahead and grab Jesus' hand. It wasn't too much later that her breathing had stopped. The nurse came in and told us she was gone.

After everyone had left the hospital to go be with more of our family, I met with the nurse. I told her that Rhonda's passing was a lot more peaceful than I thought it would be. With tears streaming down her face, she told me, "They don't happen like that. That was the most peaceful death I've ever seen." She also said, "It was beautiful how you prayed together as a family."

Val Zweber

Made in the USA
Columbia, SC
15 April 2022